ACTOR'S CHOICE:
Monologues for Teens
Volume 2

ACTOR'S CHOICE:

Monologues for Teens, Vol. 2

Edited by Sarah Bernstein & Gabriella Miyares

Playscripts
Inc.

Actor's Choice: Monologues for Teens, Volume 2 is published by Playscripts, Inc. 450 Seventh Avenue, Suite 809, New York, New York, 10123, www.playscripts.com

Cover design by Another Limited Rebellion

Text design and layout by Gabriella Miyares

First Edition: September 2012

10 9 8 7 6 5 4 3 2

Editor's Note: In some of the monologues in this book, dialogue or stage directions from the play may have been removed for clarity's sake.

Library of Congress Cataloging-in-Publication Data

Actor's choice: monologues for teens / edited by Erin Detrick.
     p. cm.
Summary: "Collection of monologues from the Playscripts, Inc. catalog of plays, representing a variety of American playwrights. The source material for each monologue may be found on the Playscripts website, where nearly the entire text of every play can be read for free. Intended for teenage actors"—Provided by publisher.
  ISBN-13: 978-0-9709046-6-9 (pbk.)
  Volume 2 ISBN-13: 978-0-9819099-9-8 (pbk.)
  1. Monologues. 2. Acting. 3. American drama--20th century. 4. Teenagers--Drama.
I. Detrick, Erin, 1981-
  PN2080.A287 2008
  808.82'45--dc22
               2007050166

ACKNOWLEDGMENTS

First and foremost, this book was made possible by all of the exceptionally talented playwrights who so generously allowed us to include their work. We are deeply appreciative.

Special thanks are due to Nathaniel Basch-Gould, Katherine Funkhouser, Kate Mulley, John O'Connor, Jason Pizzarello, and Noah Scalin for their monumental contributions to the creation of this book.

TABLE OF CONTENTS

Introduction...xi

Foreword by Jandiz Estrada xii

MALE COMEDY..1

Acts of God by Mark Rigney...2

The Bold, the Young, and the Murdered by Don Zolidis 3

The Diaries of Adam and Eve adapted by Ron Fitzgerald.................5

Firebirds by Liz Flahive...6

The Hamlet Thrill-ma-geddon by Don Zolidis............................8

Last Day at Whoopie Kingdom by Alan Haehnel........................9

Maggie by Robert Pridham 10

Mommy Says I'm Pretty on the Insides by Lucy Alibar 11

October/November by Anne Washburn......................................12

Prom Perfection by Jane Steiner...13

The Servant of Two Masters translated and adapted
      by Bonnie J. Monte 14

Spy School by Don Zolidis 15

A Tiny Miracle with a Fiberoptic Unicorn by Don Zolidis.............16

MALE DRAMA...17

4 A.M. by Jonathan Dorf 18

Confession: Kafka in High School by Bobby Keniston 20

Dracula adapted by William McNulty.......................................22

Honor and the River by Anton Dudley......................................24

Hum of the Arctic by Sarah Hammond......................................26

In Conflict adapted by Douglas C. Wager 27

Just Like I Wanted by Rebecca Schlossberg 31

Kurt Vonnegut's Slaughterhouse-Five adapted by Eric Simonson...........32

The Long View by Alan Haehnel...33

Look, a Latino! by Jorge Ignacio Cortiñas 34

The Matchmakers by Don Zolidis 35

Offerings by Alan Haehnel 36

The Other Room by Ariadne Blayde 38

Sonny's House of Spies adapted by Alec Volz 39

Spacebar: A Broadway Play by Kyle Sugarman by Michael Mitnick.......40

Striking Out the Babe by Charlie Peters...42

Voices in Conflict by Bonnie Dickinson 43

Wild Kate: A Tale of Revenge at Sea by Karen Hartman 44

FEMALE COMEDY 47

Axel F by Liz Flahive 48

*Black Butterfly, Jaguar Girl, Piñata Woman and Other Superhero
     Girls, Like Me* by Luis Alfaro...49

Chemical Bonding (or Better Living Through Chemistry)
     by Don Zolidis 50

The Diaries of Adam and Eve adapted by Ron Fitzgerald...............52

Emma adapted by Jon Jory 54

Fat Kids on Fire by Bekah Brunstetter...55

High School Musi-pocalypse by Don Zolidis...57

The Long View by Alan Haehnel 58

Maggie by Robert Pridham 59

Math for Actors by Emily C.A. Snyder...61

MilkMilkLemonade by Joshua Conkel 62

The Rehearsal by Don Zolidis 63

Seven Minutes in Heaven by Steven Levenson...64

Speed Date by Janet Allard 65

A Tiny Miracle with a Fiberoptic Unicorn by Don Zolidis...................66

FEMALE DRAMA 69

Antigone adapted by David Rush 70

Antigone Now by Melissa Cooper 71

The Audition by Don Zolidis 72

Black Butterfly, Jaguar Girl, Piñata Woman and Other Superhero Girls, Like Me by Luis Alfaro 73

Charming Princes by Emily C.A. Snyder 74

The Diary of a Teenage Girl by Marielle Heller, adapted from the graphic novel by Phoebe Gloeckner 75

Face Forward: Growing Up in Nazi Germany by Brendon Votipka 76

The Final Rose by Bekah Brunstetter 77

Hiroshima: crucible of light by Robert Lawson 78

Irena's Vow by Dan Gordon 80

Last Night in London by Kimberly Lew 82

Leah's Train by Karen Hartman 83

Patty Red Pants by Trista Baldwin 84

Perfect Score by Katie Henry 85

Regina Flector Wins the Science Fair by Marco Ramirez 86

Seven Minutes in Heaven by Steven Levenson 88

She Like Girls by Chisa Hutchinson 90

To Know Know Know Me by Courtney Baron 91

What I Want to Say But Never Will by Alan Haehnel 93

MALE OR FEMALE COMEDY 95

Darcy's Cinematic Life by Christa Crewdson 96

The Dog Logs by CJ Johnson 97

I'm Not Ebenezer Scrooge! by Tim Kochenderfer 98

Volleygirls by Rob Ackerman 99

MALE OR FEMALE DRAMA 101

Acts of God by Mark Rigney 102
Air Guitar High by Laura Schellhardt 103
Hiroshima: crucible of light by Robert Lawson 104
Just Like I Wanted by Rebecca Schlossberg 105
Rumors of Polar Bears by Jonathan Dorf 106

INTRODUCTION

Finding the perfect monologue can be a complicated task. You need a strong, juicy piece of material that will highlight your talents—preferably a piece that hasn't been seen thousands of times already. Furthermore, to fully understand the context of your monologue, you need the play itself at your fingertips to help you prepare. Often that play is impossible to track down. That's where *Actor's Choice* comes in.

We now publish over 1500 titles, many of which had not even been written when the last three *Actor's Choice* monologue collections were released. There's a wealth of engaging, dynamic monologues found within those new plays—and we're thrilled to make many of them available to you in this book.

But here's what makes *Actor's Choice* truly unique: For every monologue, you have the option of reading up to 90% of the play it comes from, all from one source, and all for free. Simply visit the Playscripts, Inc. website at *www.playscripts.com*. No longer do you have to waste time searching for a script—the work's already done for you.

On behalf of all the exceptional playwrights represented in this book, we hope that you enjoy these monologues, and that you get the part!

HOW TO USE THIS BOOK

Every monologue in this book is preceded by a brief description that introduces the context. If you'd like to read the play itself, we've made the process simple:

- Go to the Playscripts, Inc. website: *www.playscripts.com*.

- Run a search for the play title.

- Click the *Read Sample* link and read away.

- If you'd like to read the entire play, you may order a book at any time from the Playscripts, Inc. website.

FOREWORD

In my experience, 99.9 % of first time actors will mistakenly slip into the category of "boring" because they play it safe.

My advice to you is: exhaust all means within your ability to dodge that boredom bullet!

To start, you have an acute advantage to doing this. Right now, just so effortless, you are surfacing. This day and each after, you wake up a member of an entirely *au courant* voice. Generation Y: defining the "Millennials." Your advantage is youth. That curse you try so desperately to evade? It's your skeleton key to discovery, and you must use it to unlock your ferocious audition! Leap over those obvious choices and angles; instead, concentrate on finding what makes your piece so significant.

Now, significance is not reserved for the miraculous. Significance is also not owned by the privileged. Do not equate significance with what is elite or even what is rare. It may be something in a corner, shamefully unattended to…or further yet, unexamined altogether and therefore immeasurable. Give your characters your boundless attention and you will discover a significance maybe no one else has before. Even if they have, make sure no one else will transfer it to the stage like you will.

I want to leave you with a little roadmap to find your way, and discover your character's voice.

- How did your character arrive at this precise decision? This conflict? Or to this party at this moment?

- Why did the playwright choose *these* exact words over others? And how will you say these words like *no one else* will?

- Accept the challenge to develop a unique and original character.

- Discover the world and belong to it: era, demographic, comfort level.

- Commit fully using all your tools: body, voice, mask, breath.

- Start strong, finish strong.

- Inject humor where valid; even dramatic scenes can contain comedy.

- Remember onomatopoeia: you have *more* than words. Humans are animals too.

- Find the arc of the monologue—build it like a rollercoaster to ensure dynamics.

- Stay engaged, especially when you are not speaking; the strongest acting / reacting is in-between the lines.

- Beware, even in your rehearsals, the boredom bullet is on the hunt... Outrun it!

Don't be petrified, rookie. Do you have a mortgage? No? Then your greatest debt is only to yourself. Older actors can lose their magic and become blind to so much of what youthful hearts deem extraordinary. We can forget what it is to experience things for the first time: birthdays, snow, sexuality.

Do us a favor, remind us.

Jandiz Estrada

Film, television, and theater casting director
Casting department, NBCUniversal, New York City

MALE COMEDY

ACTS OF GOD
Mark Rigney

Shortly after a tornado destroys his trailer park home, Jared Seifert rediscovers his most precious possessions (his rock concert jerseys) while denying with all his might that he is failing half his classes.

JARED. So with me, it's like that John Cougar Mellencamp song, right? Life goes on. And here I am, it's a couple days later, my first day back in school, and I'm real happy, right, 'cos I found like half my concert tees out in the woods the day before, all draped over this bush, right? So I'm totally psyched, there's my Pearl Jam and Rush and Def Leppard and AC/DC—and yes! Led Zep!

(JARED *rips off the shirt he's wearing and hauls on the Led Zeppelin jersey instead, possibly getting stuck a few times along the way.*)

The genuine 100% original '74 concert jersey! Picked it up cheap on eBay. Man. Oh, sorry. I'm in school, and I was almost real late 'cos I couldn't decide which shirt to wear. It's hard, you know? It's like, my idea of Heaven is I walk in and St. Peter or whoever says, "So, would you enjoy a helping of AC/DC, or would you prefer Led Zeppelin?" and I go, "Can I maybe hear 'em both?" and he totally rocks out and says, "Yeah! Why not?" and then they jam, Led Zep and AC/DC together, for hours, with Bon Scott and Bonham back from the dead— which they aren't, exactly, 'cos in Heaven they like really are dead... Okay, sorry. I'm in school. Still. Humming that whole "Life goes on" tune, and next thing I know I get pulled right out of class 'cos I had this pre-arranged guidance counselor meeting-thing scheduled, and I'm still completely, you know, *tuned in* to the whole tornado thing, and which county my Nirvana and Billy Idol shirts wound up in, but now there's all this interference 'cos I've got Ms. Schneider on the other side of the desk asking all these not-very-nice questions, like why I'm failing algebra for the third time. But all I want to talk about is how, like, inside a tornado? I could fly. Which totally rocks.

THE BOLD, THE YOUNG, AND THE MURDERED

Don Zolidis

Valencio is the villain on the soap opera, The Bold, The Young, and The Murdered. *He is explaining his evil plans to the hero in an evil European accent.*

VALENCIO. Do you want to know? Sit. And I will explain it to you.

It began when I six. I was a little boy then. My family was poor, my father dressed us up like monkeys and made us dance in the streets. But on my sixth birthday he promised me something: he would take me to a place called the Magic Kingdom in Orlando, Floreeda. It sounded magical. Mostly because it had the word magic in its name. So we saved all of our coins, and I danced a little bit harder than ever before, and I made my squeaking noises more realistic than ever, and we saved, and we saved, and soon, we had enough money to begin our journey. On our travels my father made amusing sketches of tourists driving racecars and after only five months, we reached the magic land: Floreeda.

(He takes a dramatic stroll.)

Oh how it glorious it looked to me then. The spires of the blue castle, the robot figures of the hall of presidents, the giant chipmunk in a dress. I was in heaven. And that's when I saw him: An enormous rodent the size of my great uncle Supka, an animal so powerful he looked like a god from mythology—made flesh, with saucers for ears and a smile that could swallow the world—he looked right at me, and I was made anew. I followed him—I would have followed that rodent to the edge of the universe, but when he thought no one was looking…

(Chokes up.)

When no one was looking…He. Removed. His. Own. Head.

(He can barely continue.)

…His…Head! He was no god! He was a pimply-faced teenager! Right then and there, I dedicated my life to evil. Later that night, I gathered a small group of street urchins and we ambushed the rodent as he was returning to the castle—He was large, but clumsy, and we toppled him quickly, our tiny fists raining blows of rage upon his battered body—when he lost consciousness we tore off his head and held it aloft in triumph—my reign of terror had begun. I spent the next few days stealing purses from old ladies and used the profits to hire a gang of Albanian dock workers—we held Snow White captive for days before they gave in to our demands. Five hundred thousand U.S. Dollars and a plane ticket to Italy. I left my father there to draw sketches and dance his monkey dance. From there it was easy to become overlord of an international crime syndicate. All because of the rodent.

THE DIARIES OF ADAM AND EVE

adapted by Ron Fitzgerald

from the short story by Mark Twain

In the Garden of Eden, Adam tells God that he's grateful for all of his creations, but something seems to be missing.

ADAM. Hello God? It's me, Adam.

How's it going?

Listen, God… I don't mean to be a pest or anything. Because I really like what you've done down here. It's really…well…it's really nice. Really. I'm not pulling your leg or anything. I think it's some of your best work. Really. You got the green things…all these green…things. And the blue splashy stuff. That's fun. Tastes good too. And how about those furry guys? Huh? ROAR! Those guys are a kick in the head. And those quacky guys! And the Baaa guys…and the Mooo guys…and the…well gosh—the whole darn thing is pretty spectacular.

It's just…

Well, you see God…there's a lot of them here. I mean lots and lots of them. I mean, I am constantly stepping in something. But umm… there's only one of me. And I think I'm…I think I'm…I might be… lonely.

Lonely?

Is that a word?

> *(Lightning. Thunder. EVE.)*

Holy moo-guy!

> *(ADAM rushes off in a panic.)*

FIREBIRDS

Liz Flahive

Josh only has one thing standing between him and graduation—an incomplete in Mrs. Betensky's English class. He waits outside her house in a last-ditch attempt to convince her to give him a passing grade.

(It's nighttime. JOSH stands in front of his teacher's house.)

JOSH. Hey. I'm sorry. Look I don't make a habit of waiting outside of my teachers' houses at night. It's probably illegal or something. But I didn't want to keep the car running so I've been sitting here and...

I know I waited til the last possible moment to show any interest and take the initiative but isn't that better than just skulking off into the night? Mrs. Betensky. I've convinced everyone else that it's better if you just get me out of here. You don't want to teach me again next year. I know you don't. And I know I bailed on like every other paper and didn't rewrite this one but I read that whole stupid play again and it's not that bad.

Don't push it okay, I'm not saying I like it. I like parts of it. I mean, the whole "love makes you insane" thing, I totally get now. And that that guy Bottom is turned into an ass. I got that even though I don't think puns are funny. I still think Lysander and Demetrius are real d-bags but that's just one man's opinion. I liked Puck and I bet a lot of people aren't really into him because he's annoying. But I think he keeps everything interesting until he gets caught, you know. And that should count for something.

I know you probably don't care but I memorized this one part in case you didn't believe I actually read the stupid play. Oh. And I made this.

(He puts on a baseball cap with a bunch of leaves stuck to it. The rest of the cast quietly appears behind him. They all wear something covered with leaves.)

It's supposed to symbolize the forest and all that crap. Just, you know, visualize trees and fairies or whatever.

(Lights shift. JOSH recites Puck's final monologue:)

If we shadows have offended
Think but this, and all is mended
That you have but slumber'd here
While these visions did appear
And this weak and idle theme
No more yielding than a dream
Gentles, do not reprehend:
if you pardon, we will mend:
And, as I am an honest Puck,
If we have unearned luck
Now to 'scape the serpent's tongue
We will make amends ere long;
Else the Puck a liar call;
So (uh) good night unto you all.
Give me your hands, if we be friends,
And Robin shall restore amends.
And give me a D in your class so I can graduate

Please.

(He holds out his paper.)

THE HAMLET THRILL-MA-GEDDON
Don Zolidis

Claudius is the newly minted king of Denmark and is explaining to his subjects why the last king's suspicious death is of no concern to them at all.

CLAUDIUS. My royal subjects! I know that there have been some difficult times out there lately—we're all hurting right now after my brother's death, but this is a time for this nation to come together. Let's be honest: we all liked him. He had a great beard. I was always envious of that beard. Not so envious that I would kill, let's put that rumor to bed. My opponents out there always want to turn this into a political issue—and I think it's become a distraction for us. Read my lips: I did not have murderous relations with my brother. I'm glad we can put that issue to rest, and I hope that the people who were saying those things enjoy their time being tortured.

Now, I'm not here to talk about my personal wife, I mean life, but—again—people have been talking, so yes, I have married Gertrude. She's a stone cold fox and once she was back on the market I knew I was going to have to act fast. And some of you sickos out there think it's a little weird that I married my brother's wife two days after he died, but you should be ashamed of yourselves and you will also be tortured.

So to sum up: Time of a great personal tragedy, Gertrude is a stone cold fox, if you don't like it I hope you enjoy spikes. And I'm lowering taxes which will exempt me from any of your moral concerns forever. Now my new wife would like to say a few words.

LAST DAY AT WHOOPIE KINGDOM
Alan Haehnel

Sam discovers that the horrible job he held at Whoopie Kingdom, a second-rate amusement park, will not lead to the college scholarship he had been counting on for years. In fact, the park has been sold, and this is everyone's unexpected last day.

SAM. *(Staring straight out, trying to keep control:)* I learned in Psychology class, which I wouldn't have taken except it looked good on my transcript, that there are five stages of grief: #1. Denial, #2. Anger, #3. Bargaining, #4. Depression, and #5. Acceptance. I have moved past denial. I am no longer saying to myself, "This can't be real. I cannot have practiced four summers of soul-squashing kissing up for one goal alone, only to have it snatched away at the last moment." I'm over that stage. One down. Number three, bargaining, I'm not bothering. I'm not likely to run across and barter for my college education at a yard sale, where it sits next to some toothless grandmother's chipped porcelain elephant collection. Number four, depression? We've met. I briefly considered suffocating myself in the cotton candy machine. But that's over. That leaves number five, acceptance, which is where I need to get, and one other number. Has anyone been paying attention? Does anyone remember?

[Someone answers: "Anger."]

That is correct, John. Come here. Let me paste an imaginary star on your forehead. I wish I had one for real, but many things have turned out to be imaginary today. Many things. Here is your star. *(Grabbing the back of* JOHN's *head,* SAM *takes his thumb, licks it, and grinds the "star" into his forehead during the next lines.)* Thank-you for listening. Thank-you for paying attention. Thank-you for answering correctly with the word aaaannnngerrrr.

MAGGIE
Robert Pridham

After a series of failed daredevil stunts, Jeezer faces the possible end of his career as middle school clown.

JEEZER. *(To the audience:)* It's Joshua. Not Jeezer. Joshua Mark Willingdorf. *The Third.* I know, I know—it sort of doesn't stick, does it? I mean, do I look like a "third" to you? Soon as I hit eighteen, I'm dropping the number. But I plan to keep the Joshua part. It's a good name. Not too common. Biblical, even. I like that.

So. The "Jeezer" thing.

When I was in the sixth grade, they dared me to eat a whole package of American cheese slices I swiped from the cafeteria. 100 perfectly square, yellow slices, all in a stack. So I did. Ate the whole stack. The thing is, nobody told me there was all this paper between the slices. I just bit into the whole pile and went to town. Took forever to chew. There must have been three hundred kids standing around cheering before the teachers knew what was going on, and by the time they found out, the cheese was gone. The whole stack. With the paper. So that's it: Cheese, cheeser, Jeezer. I mean, the way I look at it, I'm the entertainment. The day I ate that cheese, I was just looking around the cafeteria and thinking, wow, it's boring as shit around here, and then somebody dared me to eat the cheese, and it just seemed like the only thing to do at the time, so I did it. Nope, nobody ever forgot about the cheese, and I had to start thinking, okay, what's better than eating 100 slices of cheese *with* the paper? What's gonna be my next big thing? Here I am, I'm fourteen and I think I've used up all of my options.

And that's bad.

MOMMY SAYS I'M PRETTY ON THE INSIDES

Lucy Alibar

Inside a truck, on a long, bleak Georgia highway. Sausage McBiscuit, a mythological Southern truck driver, explains to our gawky teenage heroine the origin of his name.

SAUSAGE MCBISCUIT.
The ladies like to call me Sausage McBiscuit.
When I was sixteen I went to Scout camp
I was a Weeblo even though I was sixteen because I wasn't good at knots
And one night as I lay on my bunk bed
The truth came crashing into me
That I was irreparably different from the other Weeblos
Because my heart was so strange and specific
so I snuck out of bed and ran twelve miles to the McDonald's
and I hid in the bathroom
and they locked me in
and I built a fort outta surplus Sausage McBiscuits.
I stuck them together with mayonnaise.
And I lived there for two days until I started to eat the fort
and they found me and I was in the paper
and after that everyone called me Sausage McBiscuit.
Now I got my own truck and it's like a fort
and I leave Sausage McBiscuit wrappers in it overnight
'cause the smell makes me feel cohesive.

OCTOBER/NOVEMBER

Anne Washburn

1982. The East Village, NYC. David is just 13.

DAVID. The big question this year was to dress up or not to dress up. Walter was all for dressing up. It's free candy, he said. It's free candy. It's worth it to be a dork for free candy. And I'm all: is it? This is in my head, not to Walter. And I'm also thinking: this might mean I'm an adult, even if my pubic hair isn't up to speed, but if it's more important to me not to be a dork, than to have a mound of free candy—and this is taking into account the near certainty that Mr. DeMarco is still in form this year, still giving away entire Hershey bars—and by not be a dork I don't mean—it's not so much about being a dork, it's about what *not* being a dork can represent which is the possibility of girls, obviously, and, more than that, the possibility of things happening. That I'm standing on the street corner, and it's almost dark, and the wind is up, and the litter is flying around, and it's exciting and that something can happen to me next, that I don't just go home, eat dinner, do schoolwork. It's hard to explain and I can't explain it to Walter who would accuse me of bending to conformity and of being afraid to be a non conformist and of course he may be *right* but it's difficult for me to believe that he's right, frankly, when he's wearing a superman outfit which is a) from Woolworth's and b) last year's and does not fit.

I know it's conformist to want truth to come from someone who looks impressive, or at least not lame.

(Quoting Walter:)

"Time to suit up Davey. The hallways are already full of cute little kids. The candy isn't going to hold out forever."

I said nah, and I stood on the street corner, and it was almost dark, and the wind was up, and the litter flying around and then I went home and ate dinner—and in my house we don't do dessert—and then did schoolwork and then went to bed.

And the next day I sat with Walter at lunch and he was loaded with candy but he didn't want to share.

PROM PERFECTION
Jane Steiner

Cory, a nervous, yet determined, young man is asking Kara to be his prom date. In his eagerness to prove that he would make a suitable date, Cory may have overthought his presentation, and in doing so, leaves Kara little opportunity to respond.

CORY. *(Clears throat.)* Kara, would you go to prom with me?

Before you answer, I do need to point out that I am fully aware that John Morris asked you yesterday. I am also fully prepared to convince you that in choosing me to be your date, *(Presents a large poster of a bar graph with the following percentages clearly labeled:)* you are 37.6% more likely to have a good time, 48.9% more likely to have your meal paid for, and 67% more likely not to be groped in the back of the limo. Unless, of course, you want that, because we could negotiate those terms under section 12B of the contract… *(Presents a thick contract and begins flipping through the pages.)*

[Kara says, "Contract?"]

Yes. All partnerships must be entered into under the best of legal scenarios. This isn't just pizza and a movie. Formalwear is involved, as well as extended curfews and slow dancing.

[Kara tries to interrupt.]

Let me just read to you from subsection 8G. It contains an outline of my business plan—I have a copy for you—for earning enough money for the price of our tickets, a suitable corsage—another negotiable item—and of course the tuxedo rental, though that contract is supplemental and provided by Bruce Formal. *(Reading:)* Party A, in agreement with Party B—

[Kara tries to interrupt again.]

If you feel uncomfortable, please take the opportunity to consult with your legal representation before signing. Of course, at seventeen, you are still a minor, so any signatures on your part must be made in the presence of a legal guardian. Oh, and the terms of the contract are valid for the next three business days.

THE SERVANT OF TWO MASTERS

translated and adapted by Bonnie J. Monte

from the play by Carlo Goldoni

The wily servant Truffaldino has just arrived in Venice with his new master and has been instructed to wait for him on the corner until his master concludes his business dealings. He shares his dismay with the audience about his new employer's lack of sense when it comes to the proper care and feeding of servants.

TRUFFALDINO. *(To audience:)* Hanging around street corners, waiting for your master, is the most boring task in the world. Not only am I bored stiff, I'm faint with hunger. We pulled into town at noon— meal time! A half hour went by, then another, then another and then my stomach started to talk to me. *(Looking at his stomach:)* He's not happy. The first thing most normal people do when they arrive in a new city is seek lodging and *food!* Then, they sit and eat the food! Not my master. He's got me hauling luggage, stopping at people's houses to deliver messages, running up stairs and down stairs and now this! Boredom and starvation. I need to talk to him about the proper care and feeding of servants. I'd be happy to serve him with love and devotion, but he's making it very hard. Here's an inn; I could pop in for a little snack, but with my luck, that's just when he'd show up looking for me. Besides, I have no money. I have nothing. I'm dying of hunger for that devil of a man, and for what? Poor Truffaldino!

SPY SCHOOL

Don Zolidis

It's 1961, and super-nerd Spencer has arrived to take the girl of his dreams out to the prom.

SPENCER. Nonsense. Prepare to have your feet swept from under you—although I must warn you that due to my asthma I am incapable of physically lifting you, and judging by your physique you're not thin enough for me to lift—I think it's important, though, that women have curves, it helps with birthing, but also, I need to prepare you—because of my acute food allergies we will not be dining at a restaurant, but instead I will prepare a sumptuous meal of peanut butter sandwiches in Ziploc bags. There may also be some gluten-free jell-o. I also feel compelled to mention that I have a sweating problem, usually it only occurs when I'm stressed out at large public gatherings, like a dance—I have a spray that I can use on my pores, but unfortunately it's a little sulfuric in nature so it accentuates my natural body odor—Also, I get vertigo sometimes in cars, so instead of driving you to the dance, I have a tandem bicycle we can ride—you can be in the back because you probably weigh more and your thighs look pretty strong, we're going to need those to go up the hill between your house and the school. Am I forgetting anything? Oh yes—if you fall in love with me, which is quite possible given my magnetism and knowledge of algebra, you're going to need to know that Wonder Woman will always come first in my heart. Okay? This is going to be magic.

A TINY MIRACLE WITH A FIBEROPTIC UNICORN
A somewhat nostalgic, sentimental comedy in two acts
Don Zolidis

Louis is a skinny eighth grader with a crush on a popular girl. He's just given her an unfortunate Christmas present and didn't get the response he wanted. He's talking to himself.

LOUIS. She's never gonna like me. She's probably gonna go out with some guy in high school who can bench press 400 pounds and has a cleft chin. Maybe if I bench pressed 400 pounds she'd like me. I could probably do it. I'd just have to spend a lot of time in the gym. Like, every day, I'll just go to the gym every day and I won't even go to school any more, I'll just work out all the time and then I'll be huge and no one will make fun of me any more. Who'm I kidding? I got a nosebleed that time I was in the gym. I never shoulda gotten her that unicorn. But she said she liked it. She didn't like it. But why would she say she liked it if she didn't like it? She's not a liar. She's a very honest person. And she was mad at her brother when she opened the door. She even smiled when she opened it. You don't just smile for no reason. She smiled at me and she took the present and she said she liked it. And I'm gonna see her tomorrow after the show. And after the show she's gonna hug me. She hugged me twice this week. I think she likes me. I can tell by the way she hugged me, that wasn't just an ordinary hug. That was like an I like you hug and I was too stupid to pick up on it. I shoulda gone in. I shoulda said, maybe we should get some coffee or something. I just totally missed my chance. Tomorrow it's gonna be different. I'm gonna kiss her.

MALE DRAMA

4 A.M.

Jonathan Dorf

Jake, mid-teens, writes a letter to a knife company–the company that sold him the knife with which he has tried to cut his wrists and take his own life.

JAKE. To whom it may concern. I recently purchased your four-inch peeling knife. It was on sale, but just because it was on sale doesn't mean it should be worse than a knife that's not on sale. Right?

(Beat.)

You advertise it as—and I quote—"the chef's ultimate weapon. The ergonomically designed handle offers maximum comfort, giving way to a razor sharp carbon steel blade." You also note that it cuts through fruits and vegetables like hot butter, standing up to the demands of the busiest professional kitchens, with no need for sharpening for three to five years. Three to five years. Not weeks. Not months. Years!

(Beat.)

I've had your knife for six days. And in these six days, I've cut a half-dozen tomatoes, two onions, one each red, yellow and orange peppers, and two cloves of garlic. Not bunches—cloves, and not even big ones—and kind of goin' soft.

(Beat.)

And therein lies our problem. Last night, I take your knife, your knife that doesn't need to be sharpened for three to five years, and thirteen vegetables later, it punks out. When it comes to two puny wrists, your razor sharp carbon steel isn't up to the job. It cuts like a butter knife, and the blood is dripping so slow it could be hours before I even lose consciousness. But my parents are the only parents I know that don't have a lethal pharmacy in their medicine cabinet, and they're out with the car, so that's not an option either, which means that now, because of your carbon-steel disappointment, I have to sit around and wait and hurt. The whole point of your knife is so I don't have to hurt anymore.

(Beat.)

Do you know what it's like to have people smear egg yolks on your lunch table just before you get there, so you don't have anywhere to sit? Don't worry—they didn't waste the whites: those went into my lunch bag. And both of those were better than the rotting mouse in my locker.

  (Beat.)

I used to cry about it. I stopped. What's the point?—unless you're too busy crying to think.

  (Beat.)

That might be something.

CONFESSION: KAFKA IN HIGH SCHOOL
Bobby Keniston

Connor K, an average high school student, wakes up in the conference room of his high school, and is accused of a crime he is quite sure he didn't commit. The only problem is, his principal, the formidable Ms. Delilse, will not even tell him what he's accused of. Now left alone after a morning of fierce interrogation, Connor releases his fears, frustation and anger to people who may not even be listening.

CONNOR. I'm not a hero! *(Pause.)* I just try to be a normal, nice guy. *(Beat.)* Hello? Hello? *(He begins to pace. He talks to himself:)* This is ridiculous. This is absurd. How is a person supposed to confess to something without knowing what they are confessing to? *(Louder:)* Clear my conscience!? Huh?! Clear my conscience of what!? CLEAR MY CONSCIENCE OF WHAT!? *(Pause.)* No, no, I'm not going to play this game, I am not going to play this game because it is not fair. *(Beat.)* It's not fair! *(Beat. CONNOR becomes more frantic.)* Please! Just tell me what I'm accused of... I can straighten this out! But I have to know what I'm accused of! *(Beat.)* I didn't do anything! SOMEONE MUST BE TELLING LIES ABOUT ME! *(Beat. CONNOR tries to calm himself down.)* No, this isn't right. I'm not going to lose it. Dignity, right, Ms. Delilse? Dignity. I can do that. *(Pause.)* After everything I've done. *(Louder:)* I've worked really hard. I keep my head down. I don't say a bad word about anyone, I get good grades. I never go to parties, I don't drink, I don't do drugs, I study... I don't get in fights, I don't do anything wrong. And for what? For what? *(Pause. Louder:)* Looks like I get punished no matter what, huh? Huh!? *(Pause.)* Confess! Confess! I sometimes tune out my parents because they are too annoying to deal with! I picked up a quarter in the hallway and kept it! The vending machine in the lobby once gave me two bags of gummy worms and I only paid for one! Are these my crimes?! I once pretended not to notice Mrs. Smith waving to me in the morning, because I didn't feel like helping her set up her classroom like I do every morning before school...I was just too tired! Is that it? Huh? Is that it!? *(Pause. Loud:)* WHY AM I HERE? *(Pause. CONNOR becomes resolute.)* I do not deserve this. Are you listening, Ms. Delilse? I do not deserve this. I am a human being who has done nothing wrong. That has to matter, that has to mean something, it just has to. Otherwise, what is the point of even coming to school, what is the point of even trying? *(He picks up one of the chairs.)* I might as well just throw this chair! Huh? I might as well give you something to punish me for, if I'm going to be punished anyway! What if I just smash this room up? Would you like that?! Would that satisfy you? *(Pause.* CONNOR *puts the chair down.)* Well I'm not going to. I know who I am. I know what I do…I know how I behave, and I do not deserve to be punished. But you know what? I don't care! You can't make me be someone I'm not, no matter what you do! I refuse! Do you hear me! I will not be your criminal, and I will not be a martyr for something I don't even know about. So you can all just forget it! I confess to nothing! NOTHING!

DRACULA

adapted by William McNulty

originally dramatized by John L. Balderston and Hamilton Deane
from Bram Stoker's world-famous novel, *Dracula*

Grief-stricken and tormented by guilt over his inability to cure his beloved Mina of the malady that has recently taken her life, Dr. Thomas Seward, in a desperate attempt to make some sense of his tragedy, begins a written description of the bizarre events immediately preceding the onset of Mina's symptoms.

SEWARD. The Journal of Dr. T.M. Seward. Entry recorded this 21st day of March, 1898. Since my last entry six weeks ago, I have seen the love of my life, Mina Grant, languish and die of a malady I could neither remedy, nor indeed diagnose. As if this were not a full enough portion of grief for any man to bear, I have subsequently been forced to witness those same symptoms developing in my dear friend, Lucy Westphal, and have been equally powerless to prevent her decline.

Though my beloved Mina's symptoms first manifested on the morning of February 7, the events of the preceding evening were so bizarre and foreboding that, although I cannot rationally connect them to our troubles, I instinctively feel they bear mentioning.

It was at dusk on that horrendous evening that I noticed a ferocious storm gathering on the horizon. The huge black cloud increased in size as it hurtled toward the shore. I know it was my imagination, but I had the distinct feeling that this was not merely some meteorological phenomenon, but rather some conscious, malevolent being with an appetite for destruction.

I was not alone in my interest since many of the villagers had gathered on the beach and at vantage points along the cliffs and were looking on in wonder and amazement, for out of the center of the storm, from the belly of the beast, as it were, a small sailing ship appeared! She was a cargo ship of the sort rarely seen any longer, and she was being tossed about cruelly like a child's plaything.

As she neared the shore, pursued by that relentless, howling maelstrom, we expected to see the frantic crewmen on deck trying to keep her afloat and guide her away from the rocks ahead. But only one figure was in evidence. There was a man at the wheel, swaying about wildly with no apparent control over his movements. Was he drunk? Unconscious? If so, how could he still be gripping the wheel?

With a crash that rivaled the thunder now all about us the ship was driven upon the rocks.

And the answer became apparent. The man was dead, quite dead. His hands were not gripping the wheel at all but had been lashed to it for reasons I cannot begin to discern.

Thinking there might still be a few living souls on board, several of the more courageous townfolk approached the vessel to affect a rescue. But, immediately, a great gust of wind tore the hatch from the cargo hold and, from below, the ship's only living occupant emerged. There he stood, impervious to the powerful winds swirling about him and the prodigious waves rushing across the deck, a huge black hound! His proportions exceeded those of any breed I had ever seen or heard of; easily larger than a Great Dane and as massive across the shoulders and haunches as a stallion. As if to acknowledge his presence, the clouds briefly parted and the full moon shown upon him prompting him to throw back his head and release a howl so loud and passionate that it could easily be heard above the winds and thunder that surrounded him. Then, with a mighty lunge, he cast himself over the rail and landed on the beach twenty feet below.

He then cast his attention to the promontory above this hospital where stands Carfax Abbey, and as he turned to gallop off in that direction he once again gave forth with that ungodly howl. This time the sound of it seemed to penetrate the very walls of the building, echoing up and down the corridors and stirring the inmates to their own wild, demonic chorus...

HONOR AND THE RIVER
Anton Dudley

Eliot has been afraid of water since his father drowned. When Honor, the most popular boy in their all-boys school, asks Eliot to row across the river to deliver a piece of sculpture he has made for his crush at the all-girls school, Eliot must overcome his fear.

ELIOT. It's evening. Seven fifteen exactly. Somewhere in the Northeastern United States, on a brisk lonely evening, a young man faces his fear.

It's dark, but Honor's sculpture will light my way. My will to cross— and its will to be taken to the place where it longs to be: both will be my guide. I begin.

It isn't that I'm a terrible rower, I'm no Honor Roberts, but I'm a lot better than I let myself believe—it's just that: fear is debilitating.

The shell launches, I feel the support of stillness drop from beneath me. Now I am floating.

I take long and narrow strokes, keeping the shell in a straight line, keeping my eyes fixed on Honor's statue. I will not look over my shoulder. I will simply row as if on a tight rope, high above some gothic circus.

It's silent; save the strange sad sound of the water's moan: a whisper that seems to come from inside me.

My hands start to shake. I am petrified of what is below me.

And I remember: I *can* swim.

I lie to myself and say I never learnt: because any memory of my father is just too painful. But he did teach me. How many people in this life truly show you their world? Trust you enough to let you in. And then that world takes him. This once magical world has grown dark and suddenly fear is everywhere. I am afraid of water, I am afraid of love, I am afraid of family: and even myself. I don't trust these things are reliable. I don't trust they will remain. I drop trust from my list of human attributes completely.

And then: Honor…he shows me his world, just the slightest peek into it, but he allows me a step inside.

And I believe in his love and this belief calms my fear.

And I begin to return.

I see that in fearing water I am actually fearing my father, and, in doing so, have lost him completely.

With my hands still shaking, I tell myself this will work. I can do this, I say. I can do this. With every stroke I take: I can do this.

Halfway across and the sky thickens, it is darker and the air grows quite cold. I breathe: the way Honor has taught me, the way I remember from class.

But my hands are still shaking.

I look down: the black mirror laughs back my reflection. Is he down there? All moving water is somehow connected and his body was never found, did it travel halfway across the world to this river? To me? "Daddy?" I call out. I see flashes of him beneath the water's surface. Gasping for breath. His body rolling helplessly beneath a crashing wave. What was in his mind? What is that moment before all is let go?

My chest contracts, the shell becomes the weight of a boulder, my arms atrophy and the oars feel as if they will swim away from the grasp of my hands. I am sweating. Panic begins to cling to my veins. "Daddy!?" I gasp, my forehead throbs, I have no idea what direction I am facing. Honor's statue at the tip of the stern seems to laugh at me. I feel sick, as if I will vomit, I bend over the side of the shell and I do not see my reflection.

I see my father. Swimming beneath the boat like a dolphin guide.

Our eyes meet and I hear music: our voices humming together. Our whalesong. He smiles and suddenly my arms are moving as wings, I glide across the surface of the river as my father leads me to safety. He is smiling and I am safe. And then he is gone. I look over my shoulder as my shell slides ashore. I have done it. I have crossed the river on my own. Love has delivered me, and now, in turn, I deliver love.

HUM OF THE ARCTIC
Sarah Hammond

Rigel, an abrasive and unsuccessful painter, has been interrupted while painting by noise from another apartment. He barges into the unknown neighbor's apartment to discover a deaf woman in a bathtub blasting Queen loud enough to shake the walls. When he realizes that his neighbor is deaf, he begins to tell her everything he has never been able to say out loud.

RIGEL. Here's the thing, it's just Queen really turns me into kind of a monster. I've been trying to capture the bricks outside the window and that music is just too...er...transcendent for me to get any real work done. I listen to a lot of blues. Small music, you know? With small sounds. That doesn't mean anything to you. Jesus. Anyway, I need to choose music that brings me down or I don't sleep at night. The way you look at me, I think I could sleep. Can you hear any of this? I can't stop talking. Look at me. Can't stop. Stop! Can't do it. See, and you can't hear a word so what's the point of all this useless...

I'm afraid of small spaces.

When I was eight I hurt my cat.

Sometimes I want to push people into the subway tracks.

I've always hated my sister. She hates me, too, and so she puts banana peels in my toilet, and I can't ever flush the toilet, and I have to go in the unisex restroom in the lobby that the bums use. We don't say these things to each other, she and I.

I never eat Chinese because the fortune cookies will tell me I'm in for a fall or life is a bad dream until you wake up, and then it's worse.

I love you.

Marry me. Will you marry me. I can't love you. I don't love you. I don't love. There. There it is.

(He covers his eyes, lets out a nervous bark.)

Whoo! You are better than a priest!

IN CONFLICT

adapted by Douglas C. Wager

based on the book *In Conflict: Iraq War Veterans Speak Out on Duty, Loss, and the Fight to Stay Alive* by Yvonne Latty

Herold is an African American Iraq War Vet in his early 20s, suffering from debilitating PTSD, unemployed, unable to work or socialize, living in Section 8 housing in the South Bronx with his wife and baby (crying offstage). There is a bottle of vodka and a glass (from which he drinks) on a small table next to him. He been drinking in order to cope, but is not drunk. Herold clearly needs to talk to someone who will really listen.

HEROLD.
One day we're drivin', right.
Alright—
we were drivin' and shit.
One of the tanks flipped over in a ditch.
So we all had to stop—
pull guard, you understand…
and secure the area.
And we're the fueler
so we had to stay in the middle
while the Bradley and the tanks,
they secure everything.
So everything's secure and blaze-blah.
I'm sittin' in my truck.
First thing you see is a crowd of people.
Now they was just standin' around waitin'.
So people get paranoid—
people in the tanks tell 'em "Back up, Back Up."

Alright—
OK—

and there's this lady walkin'
out of nowhere while we're about to pull off—
and keep on with our convoy.
And she was walkin' real slow.
So—

Read this play at www.playscripts.com

There was like—now this lady
was like closer to my truck.
Know I'm sayin'
she came out of nowhere.
So they tellin' her to stop.
So I have my M16,
I'm sayin' in Iraqi blaze-blah whatever.
She ain't want to stop,
she kept walkin'.
So nobody know if it was a bomb she straddlin'—
so shots were fired—
the lady falls—
know I'm sayin'
whatever's in her hand falls and rolls.
Nobody knew what it was—
until they see the hand of a baby come up and start cryin'.

So everybody like "Wow,"
the lady got shot in the head by mistake.
You know soldiers get paranoid
they don't know if it's a bomb,
don't want to get close to it,
close to her.
That's why I'm sayin' it was a mistake, you know—
Know I'm sayin' it was like yo—
it wasn't my fault.
I ain't know—
I didn't want to be in the middle—

So baby layin' there.
I try to walk—I—you know I was stunned.
You know I'm sayin' like "Damn."
You know I'm sayin' it's a baby,
I'm sittin' there stuck,
like, I don't know what to do.
So when I take a first step to go pick up the baby, right—
the minute I took a step to pick up this baby
another convoy zooms by and runs over the baby—
Baby was just like all tangled up, rollin'.
The head—the baby's head was just
like rollin' one direction—

the body was rollin' another direction—
Now imagine how my day was, on an everyday basis, in Iraq—
The baby's body all tangled up and just rollin'—
It was truck after truck after truck runnin' that baby over.
It was like a whole convoy of trucks and tanks
until you just seen—
Now that's—
That was sick.

You think them dreams don't—
don't—
them nightmares don't—
don't—
don't haunt me…
every day?
That shit haunts me
every fuckin' day of my life.
Know I'm sayin'
I don't know how to make it stop.
Only thing to make it stop,
see what I'm doin?
I'm drinkin' know I'm sayin—
smoke me a blunt and drink some more.
That's how I make it stop sometime.
I self medicate myself
then I go take the medication the VA gave me
and I'm knocked out.
That's how I sleep every day.
I sleep cryin' sometimes—I sleep like "Damn, for what?"
Know I'm sayin'

I imagine the guys that came home
with missing limbs and stuff like that—
imagine what they goin' through.
You may see them laughin'—
imagine what they goin through inside.
Cause they gave up a limb.
I gave up my soul.
Know I'm sayin' I gave up my-my-my
state of—the way I think.
I came back an amputee,

but you can't see my amputation.
You feel me.
My amputation is up here—
and nobody can give that back to me—
can't nobody give me a prosthetic mind or whatever.
Know I'm sayin'—
all I can do is live day by day
and wonder if I'm a die today.

JUST LIKE I WANTED
Rebecca Schlossberg

After an aggressive outburst in group therapy, and a punch in the face from one of the group members, Joey commits suicide. He explains to the audience how and why he committed the act, as well as the unexpected results of his decision.

JOEY. For the second time in my life, I attempted suicide. And for the second time in my life, along with being Hayley's older brother, I succeeded at something. That night I used a canister of sleeping pills, 27 to be exact, to kill me. Just thought you'd be curious on how I did it.

When my mom found out what happened she cried. But she always cried anyway. When my dad found out he yelled. But he always yelled anyway.

If I was aiming to change something about the way my parents acted, I didn't change a damn thing.

But I jumped out of the burning building just the same.

People'd only think about me after I was gone. That made sense to me. That was logic. After all, people only act when something happens.

One thing was clear. This time, I got myself into a hole I couldn't dig my way out of. This time, all I could do was stay in. So I buried myself inside my own hole. My own coffin. Already dug. All I did was seal it up and sleep inside it.

No more holes. Just sleep. Just like I wanted.

I'd pictured my funeral before. Dozens of times. Over and over actually. Like a record. Turns out, I was right. I was right about pretty much everything.

KURT VONNEGUT'S SLAUGHTERHOUSE-FIVE
(or The Children's Crusade)

adapted by Eric Simonson

MAN, an author, narrates a seminal event in the life of his protagonist, Billy Pilgrim, a World War II veteran who has become "unstuck in time." The event—American prisoners cleaning up after the Allied destruction of Dresden—turns out to be the start of a nervous breakdown for Pilgrim.

MAN. Billy found himself paired as a digger with a Maori, who had been captured at Tobruk. The Maori was chocolate brown. He had whirlpools tattooed on his forehead and cheeks. Billy and the Maori dug into the inert, uncompromising gravel of the moon. The materials were loose, so there were constant little avalanches.

Many holes were dug at once. Nobody knew what there was to find. Billy and the Maori and others helping them with their particular hole came at last to a membrane of timbers laced over rocks which had wedged together to form an accidental dome. They made a hole in the membrane. There was darkness and space under there. A German soldier with a flashlight went down into the darkness, was gone a long time. When he finally came back, he told a superior on the rim of the hole that there were dozens of bodies down there. They were sitting on benches. They were unmarked. So it goes.

The superior said that the opening in the membrane should be enlarged, and that a ladder should be put in the hole so that the bodies could be carried out. Thus began the first corpse mine in Dresden. There were hundreds of corpse mines operating by and by. They didn't smell bad at first—they were like wax museums. But then the bodies rotted and liquefied, and the stink was like roses and mustard gas. So it goes.

The Maori Billy worked with died of the dry heaves, after having been ordered to go down in the stink and work. He tore himself to pieces, throwing up and throwing up. So it goes. So a new technique was devised. Bodies weren't brought up anymore. They were cremated by soldiers with flamethrowers right where they were. The soldiers stood outside the shelters, simply sent the fire in.

THE LONG VIEW
Alan Haehnel

The Long View opens with a fight between Travis and Nate, Holly's former and current boyfriend, respectively. At the end of the play, we watch the fight again. This second time, we view the conflict entirely differently because we know much more about the characters—their involvement, their perspectives, even aspects of their future.

TRAVIS. I didn't mean it, when I said about how I'd rather go out with a pig than her. I didn't mean it. That sounds so stupid. It's what a five-year-old says when he does something wrong. "I didn't mean to." But this isn't like I just spilled my oatmeal or something. When I was telling her that, I was hating myself, even right while I said it, because I knew it was a complete lie. I wanted to say… I wanted to tell her, "Holly, I can't be without you! I love you more than I've ever loved anything or anyone." I wanted to say, "Please, please, please take me back."

But I couldn't. I couldn't because she finished it, right then and there, in front of everybody. She said, no matter what I did, I wasn't going to get her back. I wish she had just stabbed me right in the gut right then. I didn't know what to do, when she said that. It hurt so bad.

So I did what I always do. I got mad. And I said things that I don't believe. And the next thing you know, that kid—that Nate—he was on me and I was trying to punch his face in. But that's not what I wanted, either. It was just…something to do. When you can't possibly get what you really want, you just get mad. You just punch things. And all the time you're doing it…it doesn't help. Because the thing you really want just keeps getting farther and farther away. You feel like you're drowning—flailing around, screaming—but the boat, the one thing that can save you…it's gone. She was gone.

LOOK, A LATINO!
Jorge Ignacio Cortiñas

Enrique is Chicano, sixteen, and much to his mother's disappointment, has been arrested for shoplifting. He explains how he and his mother came to be living alone, without his father.

ENRIQUE. The last day of my father's trial went like this: We were all in that courthouse downtown, the one with windows so small they look like coin slots. My father is standing in the cold hallway outside the courtroom, this is while we're waiting for the verdict, and he's telling me Cantiflas jokes. Which irritates my Ma right, cause she's so stressed out she doesn't think this is a good time for jokes. And while my father is saying these jokes, he's emptying his pockets and giving me everything he has on him. Just in case. I'm filling my pockets with his car keys and his handkerchief and I'm listening to these Cantiflas jokes and trying to figure out what's so funny.

The trial had lasted two weeks. And during that whole trial I learnt all this stuff about my father I didn't know. Phone calls he made and people he hung out with when he wasn't with us. It was weird. And I figured if he's my father, and I don't know him, hardly at all, then for sure the jury would have a hard time figuring him out too. And to me, right there, that's reasonable doubt.

Eventually, my father ran out of Cantiflas jokes and we had to go in and listen to the white lady in the pink sweater stand up in the jury box and say, Guilty. And then the marshals came over and lifted my father up and out of his chair, by the armpits and they carried him away. I watched it all happen and there was nothing I could do. I guess, you know, that the jury people they didn't have too much reasonable doubt. Afterwards my mother and I were standing in the parking lot trying to decide who's going to drive the car home. All I had was a learner's permit, but she's like, Well, he gave you the keys so you drive.

THE MATCHMAKERS
Don Zolidis

Gabe has a huge crush on a girl that just happens to be the daughter of the guy who's marrying his Mom.

GABE. You know why I like astronomy? Because it's a study of the unattainable. And for the longest time I equated girls with the unattainable. All those galaxies out there, those stars, I'm never going to see them in person, I can only just barely scratch the idea of them in my mind, but what is important to me, what I find beautiful, is the fact that as a human being I have the chance to search out the impossible. And that's you. You are the impossible. Who would have ever thought a girl like you would like somebody like me? When I saw you in that Wendy's, I thought, I thought, that girl is a comet, and that guy she's with is a lead chain. And for the first time in my life I managed to come up and talk to you and say something. I didn't even know I could do that. But you were so amazing that you forced me to do that. To find that in myself. So I'm not gonna give up.

OFFERINGS
Alan Haehnel

Micky and his companions—all strangers to one another—have been summoned by a mysterious entity promising that, if they bring the right item, it will be accepted. Precisely what acceptance means or what criteria are required to gain it, no one knows, but that does not keep them from seeking it. Micky chooses to bring a shell he found at a yard sale; he spins an elaborate lie about it.

MICKY. Don't mind if I do. This, as you can see, is a conch shell. Now, the thing about this conch shell is that it's been in my family for years. My great-grandfather, Isaac Turner Newman, found it on the beach in Nova Scotia when he was just eight years old. As the story goes, he picked up the shell and put it to his ear, like everyone does with shells like this, and he heard the ocean. Of course, he was right next to the ocean when he first listened, but old Isaac kept listening, over and over, even when he had left the seashore and returned to his native home in West Kensington, Ohio. And he kept hearing the ocean, all right, but he also began to find that he could hear other things from this shell—he claimed he could hear the whisper of great possibilities to come. He had a special girlfriend of his listen and he asked her if she could hear wedding bells and the sound of laughing children. She swore she could. They later married and had nine children—one being my grandmother, Sarah Newman. Old Isaac took his conch shell to a friend of his and asked him if he could hear the sound of giant machinery and factory whistles. The friend said he could, just faintly, and he and my great-grandfather started what turned out to be one of the most successful machine shops in all of Ohio. From generation to generation, this conch shell has been a guide for our family. Business ventures, relationships, investments, dreams of all kinds have been tested. It's become part of our family's special language, in fact. Only half-joking, we say: Have you consulted the conch? I've heard that all my life at family reunions and gatherings: Have you consulted the conch? So what do I hear when I put this special shell to my own ear? *(He does so.)* I hear, first, nothing. Slowly, the sound of waves begin to emerge, as if from behind a muffling bank of fog. But if I listen ever so carefully, I can hear the whispers of what I might become: the sound of a bat hitting a ball, the sound of someone reading the names of graduates, and other sounds I cannot yet make out but know I someday will be able to. Is this shell an oracle, a prophet declaring what absolutely will come to us? No. Perhaps my great-grandfather never heard a thing echoing in its chambers. But when I put it to my ear, I can feel the confidence of my family, the support of those who believe in me. The sound of love. And more than anything, that is what will bring me, and all of us, a successful future. That was about two minutes, wasn't it?

THE OTHER ROOM
Ariadne Blayde

Austin, a brilliant teenage astronomer with autism, has just met Lily, a pretty girl who already seems to understand him better than most of his classmates. He tells her of the world he longs for, in which his autism isn't seen as his defining characteristic.

AUSTIN. Sometimes I go back to Schrodinger's cat but take it even further and imagine that at every moment the universe splits into an infinite number of parallel universes where anything could happen and everything could be completely different than it is in this one… like shrimp wouldn't exist and you would be a professional ping-pong player and we would call chairs "flumwangles" and… I wouldn't— I would be…

(A pause. There is deep gravity in the room.)

But most people are afraid of infinity. They think space is empty and distant because it doesn't make sense to them and it seems so different from what they're used to. But they forget that this planet is only a part of space, not separate from it and they're the ones missing out because when they think of space as frightening and empty it's really just a reflection of their world. They don't see space as a possibility, they see it as an empty void and that's what I don't understand.

(A beat.)

Because for me it's different because space is where I would feel comfortable. It's here that is a void.

SONNY'S HOUSE OF SPIES
adapted by Alec Volz

based on the book by George Ella Lyon

Alabama 1955: White thirteen-year-old Sonny has just returned from visiting his African-American maid's daughter Nissa, who is recovering in the hospital after having her leg amputated. Sonny is confused about these new feelings he has for this girl—or any girl, but especially a girl from a completely different world.

SONNY. Talking to Nissa really got me confused. First there was feeling like I'd lost something when I left the hospital. But I figured I was just shook up from seeing a young person in that kind of flux. Then later in the evening, I tried to go back to our talk in my mind. It wasn't finished somehow, but I didn't know what to do with it. What did "I just about like you" mean? What about the way she laughed? What about the damp heat of her back I hadn't meant to touch? What about her being there at all, Mamby's daughter, with *me,* and that awful emptiness that had been her leg? Why was I thinking like this? I was hoping Mama would go back to see Nissa and ask me to go with her, but she didn't. Once it looked like Nissa was doing okay, Mama slid back over the line. The line you can't see that cuts off Mamby and Nissa's life from ours. Mamby crosses that line to come here, but maybe it's okay to cross in that direction. Or maybe it's because she gets paid. *(To MAMA:)* Mama why is it that Mamby comes here but we never go to her house?

SPACEBAR: A BROADWAY PLAY BY KYLE SUGARMAN

Michael Mitnick

Kyle is a 16-year-old Coloradan playwright who has arrived in NYC to follow his destiny. A long time ago, his older sister Danielle died. He's never gotten over it. Kyle doesn't know anyone in the city. His crush, Jessica, has come to Manhattan with her family for winter break. Kyle confides in Jessica what he's been doing with his time.

KYLE. After…after rehearsals, I don't have anything to do.

And I have nowhere to go.

And I don't know anyone.

So I've just been walking around the city.

I haven't taken the subway once. It's too confusing anyway.

So I've just been walking around the city.

I had a sister once. Her name was Danielle.

I remember she always said she wanted to live in New York.

"Someday."

Danielle slept with a nightlight. She was older than me and I didn't even sleep with one because I wanted to be, well, I wanted to be "a big boy."

I used to make fun of her. She said she wanted to live in New York because the skyline out her window would be her nightlight.

She said someday she'd move to the city and get a dog and run a big restaurant where everyone tries to eat but can't get a reservation.

(KYLE smiles to himself.)

I've been walking around the city.

And I look into the apartment windows of the brownstones on the Upper West Side and I think, "Would this be Danielle's apartment?" With the dark green walls and dark wooden furniture. No, she'd be much too cool for the Upper West Side.

So I walk around SoHo and then the East Village and look into those windows.

"Would this be Danielle's apartment?"

And sometimes I see a boy through the window who's around twenty maybe. And he looks nice. And cool. And I think, "Maybe this would be her apartment and this guy would be her boyfriend."

So then I walk around the city some more.

And I see restaurants where she'd have jobs, trying to work her way up. And I see the dogs in Washington Square Park and I pick out the one that would be hers.

And I walk some more and more and more and I see the shops where she'd shop and the cafes where she'd read and the bar where we'd have a glass of champagne to celebrate the opening of my play and the more I walk, the more I start to see, in the distance, maybe a block or two up from me, a head. A head set apart from the crowd.

A head with long, brown hair.

And I watch as the head turns to the side and laughs.

And I think that maybe…it's Danielle.

And that maybe she's here.

And that maybe she's happy.

> *(Silence.)*

But then I remember that it's not Danielle.

And I wish that that girl up the block were the one who was dead.

Instead of my sister.

STRIKING OUT THE BABE
Charlie Peters

In this monologue a boy tells his family of his dream to pitch in the big leagues. But his grandmother warns him that others have dreams, too, and in those other dreams the boy could find himself in a role he wouldn't have chosen to play.

(Lights come up on CHARLIE.)

CHARLIE. I used to go to my grandparents' house every Sunday for chicken supper. After supper, my mother would tell me to tell my grandparents what my plans were, my dreams. I'd tell them my plan was to become a big league baseball player, a pitcher for the Cubs, and I wanted throw the fastest fastball, the meanest curve, and a change up that would stop half way to the plate before starting up and going again. I told them I'd win more games and strike out more batters than Cy Young and I would be loved by the fans. Not just admired, I'd be loved. I would be adored. Every Sunday, as soon as I finished outlining my dreams, my mother would say "Isn't it wonderful that Charlie has a dream?" And my grandfather would smile and agree, and my grandmother would say the same thing.

(As GRANDMOTHER*:)* Every dream has an asshole. Don't you end up being the asshole in no other man's dream.

(After a pause.) It was not the support a young boy yearns to hear. But she loved me and it was her way of looking out for me.

(Blackout.)

VOICES IN CONFLICT
Bonnie Dickinson
and the theatre students of Wilton High School;
based on the true experiences of soldiers in their own words

An veteran of the Iraq war reflects on his deployment in this piece, based on the true experiences of soldiers in their own words.

BRIAN MOCKENHAUPT. I've spent hours taking in the world through a rifle scope, watching life unfold. Women hanging laundry on a rooftop. Men haggling over a hindquarter of lamb in the market. Children walking to school. I've watched this and hoped that someday I would see that my presence had made their lives better, a redemption of sorts. But I also peered through the scope waiting for someone to do something wrong, so I could shoot him. When you pick up a weapon with the intent of killing, you step onto a very strange and serious playing field. Every morning someone wakes wanting to kill you. When you walk down the street, they are waiting, and you want to kill them, too. That's not bloodthirsty; that's just the trade you've learned. And as an American soldier, you have a very impressive toolbox. You can fire your rifle or lob a grenade, and if that's not enough, call in the tanks, or helicopters, or jets. The insurgents have their skill sets, too, turning mornings at the market into chaos, crowds into scattered flesh, Humvees into charred scrap. You're all part of the terrible magic show, both powerful and helpless. I miss Iraq. I miss my gun. I miss my war.

WILD KATE

Karen Hartman

inspired by Melville's *Moby Dick*

Piper is shy, but he's gained a new confidence at High School on the High Seas, a program where misfit high school students spend a semester on a boat. Inspired by Wild Kate, their mad captain, he offers a fresh perspective on Moby Dick *in his oral report.*

PIPER. The nature of *Moby Dick.* By Piper, for credit in language arts.

What they tell you the book is about, it's *not* about. This is the only way a book so massively colossal could ever be considered boring by my peers.

> *(The boat hits a wave and rocks.)*

I Wikied it too, last year in AP English Lit. Because my teacher said it was a story of revenge, and gave all these essay topics about Ahab and the whale. Yet Ahab doesn't show up until more than a hundred pages in, and then more or less just yells, "Hast seen the white whale?" and goes back into his forecastle or whatever. Then there's a monstrous bloody climax. Which rocks.

But I think this is a story of witnessing. Making sense out of violence, not apologizing, just asking for real:

Where are we in the food chain?

What is the meaning of a culture fueled by dirty oil, obtained by barbaric means?

If corpses power our civilization, are we civilized?

I had the chance to think about this at the feet of a person asking the big asks. Captain Kate squints into the sun, and *moves us out.*

Kate says Herman Melville never had an education. He was orphaned at twelve and went to work, got a job on a whaling vessel.

> *[Someone says: "No shit?"]*

Check this. It's the narrator Ishmael but it might as well be Herm Melville himself:

(Reads:)

"And as for me, if, by any possibility, there be any as yet undiscovered prime thing in me; if hereafter I shall do anything that, upon the whole, a man might rather have done than to have left undone; if, at my death, my executors, or more properly my creditors, find any precious manuscript in my desk, then here I prospectively ascribe all the honor and the glory to whaling; for a whale-ship was my Yale College and my Harvard."

Really gives a person perspective about college applications.

FEMALE COMEDY

AXEL F

Liz Flahive

Ethel is unhappy about her father's second marriage, but when called upon to make a wedding toast, she has to find something to say to him.

ETHEL. Hey. Helloooo. So. I'm going to wing it because I'm the irresponsible daughter without a job. Uhm. So. My dad and I hated each other from like 1984-1992. Now I think he's a lot nicer because he still pays my car insurance.

So. For all of you I don't know and uhm, new step family people or whatever, I wanted to tell you a little something you might not know about my dad. Yeah. When I was little, I had a lot of problems or whatever and on top of everything, wouldn't go to sleep. And I'd crawl into my parents' bed but I was like 11 or 12 and totally too old for that. Mostly I wanted to wake up my mom because if I did she'd take me downstairs and watch TV with me. But she was sick at that point so… So my dad would wake up and walk me back to my room. Like right away. No "Do you need a drink of water or…" And I told him I wouldn't go to sleep unless he sang me a song and, shit, okay, some Background! The other thing I hated about my dad is that he didn't like anything I liked. He never listened to music. He only read non-fiction.

Anyway. The next night I was being an asshole and trying to wake up my mom and he grabbed my arm and walked me back to my room. And he sat down next to my bed and he sang me this song. Because that's the kind of guy my dad is. He taught himself a song because I told him I needed it to sleep. And tonight. I'd like to play it for him. And his new…lady.

BLACK BUTTERFLY, JAGUAR GIRL, PIÑATA WOMAN AND OTHER SUPERHERO GIRLS, LIKE ME

by Luis Alfaro

based on the writings of Alma Elene Cervantes, Sandra C. Muñoz, and Marisela Norté

Sylvia shares an experience she had growing up.

SYLVIA. Today, my *Ama* bought a set of mattresses for me, because the ones I sleep on squeak a lot… and have really big yellow pee stains too. So my mom has been thinking all day what she should do with the old ones.

She finally decided she would burn the mattresses in the back yard.

I told her I didn't think she could do that, but she said that when she was in *Mexico,* her *Papa* used to burn their trash in the backyard all the time. So my mom and me, carried the mattresses and put them where there were hardly any trees around. My mom threw a match on the mattresses, and before we knew it, they were burning real fast and the flames kept getting bigger and bigger.

We just stood there looking at the fire, when we heard fire engines coming up the alleyway behind our house. My mom just kind of looked at me, like she didn't understand what was going on, because the firemen *couldn't* be coming to our house.

But before she could say anything, a bunch of firemen, in puffy yellow suits, climbed the back wall with big axes, and a hose a lot bigger than the one we were holding. They started putting out the fire and pushing us out of the way.

My mom started yelling at *me* in Spanish to tell them to stop, but I wasn't going to tell those men anything. Plus, they were looking at us like we were stupid. It didn't help that my Mom was wearing her pajamas and I was wearing my Halloween *Princess Leia* costume I had just put together that morning.

Afterwards, the firemen made me tell my mom, in Spanish, that she shouldn't be burning mattresses in the backyard.

But she didn't really understand what the big deal was.

They were her mattresses and her backyard!

CHEMICAL BONDING
(or Better Living Through Chemistry)
Don Zolidis

Dani has just graduated from high school as salutatorian and has been forced to give a graduation speech. She's pretty nervous and not terribly good at it.

(DANI stands behind a small podium. She is dressed in a blue graduation gown, with mortar and cords. She reads from note cards and looks up haltingly. She's not the best speaker in the world.)

DANI. Congratulations class of 2010! *[Or whatever graduation year it is currently.]* We have officially made it! Thirteen years, and for some of us, more, I'm talking to you Jacob, have culminated in this moment. I never thought I would be standing here today. When one thinks about education, one is often struck by how…I believe it was Plato who said "the unexamined life is not worth living."

(She looks out to the audience.)

That was Socrates? Socrates. Okay. To be fair, I didn't say it *was* Plato, I said I *believed* it was Plato, there's a difference. Well I am not a good comment on the American educational system apparently. Back to my speech.

(She looks down at her note cards again.)

I believe it was *Socrates* who said "the unexamined life is not worth living" and we have been examined a lot. From standardized tests in fourth grade, to standardized tests in fifth grade, to that mile time trial we all had to do in sixth grade, to standardized tests in seventh grade… we have been examined. And what have we learned? Well…

(She looks down at her cards again.)

Actually I'm not going to read this. This speech is terrible. They made me write this in my communications class and it's awful. I just wanna talk to you, okay?

(Pause. She tries to think of something to say.)

You ever do that? You ever think you've got something deep to say and then it turns out there's absolutely nothing in your brain? I just had that moment and I am beginning to freak out. Um…but…getting on with it. Graduation. Crap. Is anybody else out there like totally terrified? I know I shouldn't because I'm like salutatorian and all; I would have been valedictorian except for Mr. Jackson's long-term sub, but I'm not going to get into that. But it's like: part of me just wants to stay in homeroom forever, you know? And then part of me is like, no, you should burn everything to the ground and then spit on the ashes, you know? I'm not going to do that, Officer Weeks. I'm totally over that.

But um…we're done with high school. And we're moving on. Yeah.

(She stands there.)

So okay that wasn't better than what I had on the cards. Do I have time to do that over?

THE DIARIES OF ADAM AND EVE
adapted by Ron Fitzgerald
from the short story by Mark Twain

Newly created Eve has just discovered that she loves to talk and that she has someone that she can talk to—Adam. She decides to try out her new skills.

EVE. The moon got loose last night. Did you notice? It slid down and fell out of the sky. A very great loss. It breaks my heart to think of it. Does it break your heart? To think of it? It breaks my heart to think of it. It should have been fastened better. I wonder if we can get it back again?

(ADAM opens his mouth to speak, but EVE goes right on.)

Of course, there's no telling where it went. And I'm sure whoever finds it will hide it. I know I would. Not that I'm a dishonest person. I'm honest. Mostly honest. More honest than most. But I have come to realize that the core and center of my nature is a love of beautiful things. And shiny things. I love the beautiful shiny things. I have an overwhelming passion for beautiful shiny things. So it probably would not be safe to trust me with a moon that belonged to someone else.

(ADAM tries to get a word in. And fails.)

I could give up a moon that I found in the daytime. Because I'd be afraid someone was looking. You ever get the feeling that someone is watching you? Just hovering about watching your every move?

(ADAM shoots her a look.)

Yeah, like that. But if I got a hold of a moon in the dark…forget it. I'd find some excuse not to say anything to anyone about it. Because I just love moons. They're so pretty and so romantic and so beautiful and shiny. I wish we had five or six of them. I'd never go to bed. I'd never get tired of lying on the moss-bank, looking up at them.

(EVE is lost in her reverie. ADAM notices the silence. He wants to say something, but thinks it may be a trap. He regards her with suspicion. She doesn't seem to notice him. Finally, he readies himself to speak.)

Stars are good too. I wish I could get some to put in my hair. I can't seem to reach them. You'd be surprised to find how far off they are. They sure look close enough. I tried to knock some down with a pole. That didn't work. Then I tried throwing rocks at them. That didn't work either. I think it's because I'm left-handed and can't throw so good. Even when I aimed at the one I wasn't after, I couldn't hit the other one. Though I did make some close shots. I think. Because I saw the black blot of my rock sail right into the middle of those golden clusters like forty or fifty times. I kept just barely missing them. So I cried a little, which is natural, I guess, for someone my age. And then I got a basket and headed for a spot on the far edge of the circle, where the stars were close to the ground and I could get them with my hands, which I figured was better anyway because then I could gather them tenderly instead of smashing them with a rock. But the edge was a lot farther away than I thought and I got tired of walking and so I had to give up. I found some tigers and snuggled in with them. It was very comfortable. And their breath was fantastic because they live on strawberries. I'd never seen a tiger before, but I knew them in a minute by the stripes.

EMMA

adapted by Jon Jory
from the novel by Jane Austen

Emma Woodhouse is an avid matchmaker who has no interest in marriage for herself, but when handsome Frank Churchill becomes infatuated with her, she must decide what to do about his show of affection.

EMMA. Well. He is more in love with me than I supposed. A few minutes more and there is no telling how it might have ended. I am sure he almost told me that he loved me. And I think I must be a little in love with him. This sensation of listlessness, weariness, stupidity, this disinclination to sit down and employ myself, this feeling of everything being dull and insipid about the house... I must be in love. But, on the other hand, I cannot admit myself to be unhappy. I can imagine him to have faults and I must say that the conclusion of every imaginary declaration on his side is that I refuse him. Perhaps I am not in love for I do suspect that he is not really necessary to my happiness. He is undoubtedly very much in love, everything denotes it. When he comes again, I must be on my guard not to encourage it. His feelings are warm, but I can imagine them rather changeable. Hmmm. Every consideration of the subject, in short, makes me thankful that my happiness is not more deeply involved. I shall do very well again after a little while and then it will be a good thing over; for they say everybody is in love once in their lives and I shall have been let off very easily.

(Struck.)

I wonder if Harriet could not succeed me in his affections. He calls her my 'beautiful little friend.' How advantageous it would be to Harriet! I must not dwell upon it... I must not think of it. I know the danger of indulging such speculations.

FAT KIDS ON FIRE
Bekah Brunstetter

Nurse Joy welcomes campers new and old to New Image Camp Vanguard, and sets the ground rules for campers. The stakes are particularly high this year, considering the camp might close after this summer.

NURSE JOY. You have no idea how much joy it brings me to welcome you to New Image Camp Vanguard. So much Joy, it's sad.

Welcome, old! Welcome, new, to a journey, to say the least. A journey towards self-improvement and self-discovery.

(Pause.) But in terms of self-discovery, campers, please keep this discovery to your selves. You will find that self-discovery-ing your fellow campers in the gazebo will distract you from the task at hand.

Our goal here over the next six weeks is to re-invent the way to think about food, exercise, and your physical person. While engaging in fun and rewarding group activities, unbeknownst to you entirely, you will also be shedding pounds!

There is nothing more important than being physically fit—socially, emotionally. But even more so—we will help you find your beauty WITHIN. I've found mine—can you find yours?

My name is Joy— I'm the nurse and the dietician— This is my eleventh year. I am also a veteran and proud graduate.

I spend the off season an hour North outside of Orlando. I have two cats, Rodgers and Hammerstein. I am not lonely at all. I enjoy reduced fat sour cream and the wedding channel.

> *(Pause. No one is paying attention.)*

This first week is crucial. No slip-ups. Counselors—like Mark—

> *[Indicates MARK.]*

Will be checking your bags and person regularly for forbidden paraphernalia. Cool Ranch Doritos, Little Debbie Nutty Bars, Fritos, Rolos, butterscotch chips, marmalade, three layer dips, microwavable breakfast burritos, bunny bread, potted meat, any and all Chef Boyardee products. What is hunger? Is it boredom?

NO CHEATING.

Weigh in happens every Sunday. You will take your meals, three a day, in the cafeteria. Your days will be strategically and lovingly arranged by yours truly, with aerobics in the morning, soccer and swimming in the afternoon, cooking and entertainment in the evening. If you're theatrically inclined, auditions for *A CHORUS LINE*—

   [Interrupted by a squeal.]

Uh—A Chorus Line—will be held this evening in the Rec Hall. Counselor Stevens will direct.

Step lightly, children. Mind your counselors—be proud of who you are. Stay hydrated.

   (Suddenly serious.)

And No monkey business. I don't want to see a single—not like last year. No pranks, no jokes, no pregnancies, no smoking in the shower. Broken ankles, acceptable. Keep it in your pants.

   (Suddenly British, perhaps.)

This is a *civilized* establishment.

HIGH SCHOOL MUSI-POCALYPSE
Don Zolidis

Alejandra, an actress, is sharing an emotional memory with her acting class in order to access her sadness.

ALEJANDRA. I had all the Barbies. I had Career Barbie and Workout Barbie and Regular Barbie and the house and the car and everything. And I used to act out little scenes with them; like all the Barbies lived in one big house together—I didn't have Ken, I hated Ken, but all the Barbies lived in the dream house and they used to have tea together and Career Barbie used to make Regular Barbie clean the house and cook dinner and everything. Workout Barbie didn't care, she was always in front of the television and Regular Barbie had to do all the work. They were so mean to her. Career Barbie would come home and she'd say, "I'm putting food on the table! I break my back every day, the least you could do would be to have a hot meal ready for me when I get home!" and then Regular Barbie would cry and Workout Barbie would just keep working out. She was obsessed. And then I remember…my older brother Jared—he used to have his G.I. Joes come over and pop off the Barbies' heads. So one day I went up to my room and Regular Barbie was gone. And I thought, she's had enough, she's left Career Barbie and Workout Barbie and has gone off to be a meteorologist. I used to love meteorologists until I discovered they were liars. So Career Barbie looked everywhere and she was really sad and she said, "Please come back! I'm sorry I was mean to you! I promise to do my share of the housework!" but Regular Barbie didn't come back. And Workout Barbie was just doing aerobics like the stupid bimbo she was. So Career Barbie went a little crazy. We looked everywhere together. And then we found her. Jared's G.I. Joes had tied her to a stick in the backyard and were shooting firecrackers at her. They had a little cannon set up and everything. Her whole left side had melted down. Career Barbie cried and cried and we took her down from the stick and set her up in the bed in the dream house and then Career Barbie made the dinner and cleaned the house too. Workout Barbie kept on doing aerobics because she was heartless. But Career Barbie felt really sad. And then the story has a happy ending because Career Barbie learned not to take Regular Barbie for granted and also I took Jared's G.I. Joes and ran them over with the lawnmower.

THE LONG VIEW
Alan Haehnel

The Long View opens with a fight between two boys, a fight that we eventually see from various perpectives. Here Hanna, a classmate of the boys, reflects on the day of the fight.

HANNA. I want life to be fair. Is that so much to ask?

That day…that was a very bad day for me, all things considered. My brother ate the last of the Cocoa Puffs and drank the last of the milk at breakfast—both unfair events because I was the one who went to the store and bought those items when they ran out the last time. First period, Mr. Collesco marked me tardy, which, I admit, I was, but so was Rebecca Halloren, even more tardy than I was, but Mr. Collesco happened not to be looking when she snuck in, so she didn't get marked late. And then, unfairness to top all unfairness, Ms. Moore, that lovely Geometry teacher of mine, decided that the questions on this extremely-heavily-weighted test she invented should have nothing to do with the homework we had been doing for the past two weeks leading up to said test! Unfairness bothers me.

So normally, if some boy Bozo—and generally, all boys are Bozos—decided he wanted to fight some other boy Bozo, and the first Bozo was clearly more qualified to pound the stuffing out of the second Bozo—in other words, if the match of the Bozos was completely unfair—normally, I would not have cared. But that day, I could not keep myself from taking a stand, to try to diminish, just slightly, the lack of equity in my world. And what did I get for my efforts? Sarah Dobson—whose nose rarely drops below an upraised angle of 120 degrees (I am very good at Geometry, by the way)—Sarah chooses to call me a stuck up witch! And I didn't even get a chance to pull her hair out! *(Whispered:)* Unfair.

MAGGIE
Robert Pridham

After a particularly difficult classroom encounter with a troubled student, Ms. Wither recalls an unsettling seventh grade memory of her own.

MS. WITHER. *(To the audience:)* When I got to the seventh grade, I wanted to have Mrs. Latcher for science. Everybody knew Mrs. Latcher, and everybody wanted to be in her class. Mrs. Latcher melted sugar in test tubes and made candy in her class. She burned sulfur to make the whole second floor smell like rotten eggs. She mixed secret chemicals together to cause an explosion right on her desk. She had three guinea pigs in her classroom, four turtles, and an iguana named Iggy Pop. She told jokes and she wore jeans and somebody had even seen her shopping at the mall—with her husband, who was very handsome and was probably a famous movie star. Everybody said so. Once, when she dropped a tray of test tubes on the floor, she said "Shit!" right out loud in front of the whole class, and then she laughed, and then everybody laughed.

She was utterly and completely cool.

One day, in the middle of class, she was talking to us about action and reaction, about energy, about how every cause has an effect, and all of a sudden she shouted "Stop! Don't anybody move!" We all froze. "Now stand absolutely still!" she said. And we all stood absolutely, completely, impossibly still. I was even trying not to breathe—I didn't want any part of my body to be moving at all. The whole class was motionless. And that's when she said "Do you know how fast you're going right now?"

I didn't know what she was talking about. She'd just asked all of us to be as completely still as we could be, and I thought I was doing a pretty good job.

"Right now," she said, "at this very moment, even though you think you're standing perfectly still, you're going 1080 miles a minute. That's how fast the earth is moving around the sun. That's how fast *you* are moving. And not just around the sun. You're also moving through space. The very ground you're standing on right now, right this very minute. And do you know how fast the ground is going? The ground is going 11,180 miles a minute."

I couldn't breathe. I started to imagine how fast that really was, how fast I was going, spinning, racing through space, even though I thought I was standing completely still. I started to think I could feel the wind in my hair, and my cheeks getting tighter and tighter, and my eyelids peeling back and all of the tears being blown right out of my eyes and my arms getting pushed back behind me because I was going so fast that I couldn't even keep up with myself.

I couldn't stop thinking about it. I kept looking around, up, down, on my way home from school, in my room at night, just waiting for the huge, speeding blast of wind to roar up out of nowhere and rip me out of my chair and send me spinning off into empty, empty space.

I hated Mrs. Latcher after that.

MATH FOR ACTORS
Emily C.A. Snyder

Kate, a serious math tutor, attempts to tutor a full-of-himself actor, Keith, who is always late. He's wearing tights, he's more interested in her love life than in limits, and he probably hasn't done his homework again. But Kate has a dramatic plan of her own to find a common denominator.

KATE. You know, I had really hoped, I had *really* hoped that you had changed. Everyone told me not to take you on as your math tutor, you know. Everyone said, "Kate, don't you take him on! Just because he's charming and handsome and debonair, don't be fooled into thinking a common...*thespian*...cares a bit about math!"

Take on an artist, they said. An artist will just draw at you. Take on an English major. They'll understand iambic pentameter. Take on an historian! The Norman Invasion of 1066! The War of 1812! It's a walk in the park with a History major. *Anyone* but a theatre person.

But I said, "No, I've known Keith since we were kids. And, sure, he used to smile at me...uh, the *girls* and get them to do his math homework, but did you see him in last year's play? He's so grown up! He'll do the work."

But *no.* You haven't changed a bit. I'm so sick of all you actors with your *excuses* and your *drama* and your *feelings* and your—what are you doing?

MilkMilkLemonade
Joshua Conkel

Linda is a chicken scheduled to be processed by The Machine, a steel monstrosity that will turn her into nuggets. As she hides under the porch waiting for a secret rendezvous with her only friend, she reflects on her brief life and how a small change in attitude can change the course of one's life. Also, she has a Brooklyn accent.

LINDA. Sure is friggin' creepy here beneath the porch. I don't like all these spider webs. *(Beat.)* I wonder if I'm feeding into the stereotype of chickens being cowardly, or do you think it's simply normal to be frightened in a situation like the one I currently find myself in? I mean, the thing about being a chicken is that there's very little in the way of spontaneity. Mostly things just trudge on in the same way. No surprises. You kind of get used to it after some time, and you think, this is how my life will proceed. On a straight line, in measurable increments, until I die. Until I go into the machine, which is my manifest destiny. And then something happens, and it's like, "oh. there's all these other things I can do." And it's strange and sort of scary, but for the first time you feel sort of hopeful. For the first time you feel something that's not just a sort of dull contentment. And it's nice. Scary and nice. *(Something comes over her and she clucks loudly. She reaches beneath her and pulls out an egg:)* I just laid an egg!

THE REHEARSAL
Don Zolidis

Morgan is the super-enthusiastic star of the theatre program. She's only a little bit bitter that she has the second-best part in the show.

MORGAN. Hi everyone! You know me! I'm Morgan Hill, and I'll be playing the part of Miss Sarah Brown, which is the second most fun part in the play, next to the other lead, Adelaide. I don't mind, though, because I really like wearing starchy costumes and having my hair in a bun. And also awesome! I get to kiss Barry in this show, which I've really been looking forward to for a while because that's totally what I thought I'd be doing with my life at this point! Not that I'm bitter! I'm not bitter! I love my part! I love singing really high and showing no emotion on stage! By the way, I wanted to do *Wicked,* which is an incredibly awesome show and I would have made the best Elphaba ever—can I just do a little bit of my audition song?

> *(She starts in on her audition song. MR. HENDERSON tries to cut her off, but she won't let him. She finishes.)*

But that's cool. Apparently, we don't have the right to do that show or something—so instead we're doing this show, which is just great, which is awesome, cause instead of flying and singing amazing songs, I get to be Miss Sarah Brown—who is working for the Salvation Army, can you believe that?! How much fun is it to work for the Salvation Army and ring that bell! Much more fun than flying and using magic, I can tell you that much! And I think this is the year that Barry learned what deodorant was, so that's a bonus! And it looks like some of his pimples are clearing up, double bonus! I can't wait to do this show!!!! *(She takes a deep breath.)* I am a team player.

SEVEN MINUTES IN HEAVEN
Steven Levenson

Margot, an earnest but insecure high school freshman who spent the summer working as a camp counselor, relives the magic night she spent with fellow counselor Mike.

MARGOT. Then suddenly it's August.

It's the last day, it's Tuesday. And we're walking, the campers are sleeping, it's nine o'clock, it's Tuesday, and we go for a walk, there's free time for an hour, and we go for a walk for an hour.

There's a million, there are all of these, there are ten million fireflies everywhere.

The grass was wet. He said something about how, what shampoo did I wear or how it smelled like it was… I couldn't even, my heart started— was it apple or was it, and I was, green apple, yeah.

He took my hand. His hand was smaller than I thought it would be. His fingers were long but his hand was small. It was soft and wet, warm. He laughed, he was sorry his hands, he said, when he got, he was nervous.

We sat down. I held my knees against my chest like this, like I was holding them right there. I was trying to be normal, act normal, his hands were, act normal, we sat there, the grass was wet, act normal, it was through my shorts, up into my shorts, something was biting my leg, act normal, he didn't say anything but I wondered about his shorts, I wondered what he was, if I could just act normal, something kept biting, act normal, my shorts were, my knees were, his fingers, everything, then everything, everything started to, everything was, and then. Then we. And then it was. Then it. And then.

(Pause.)

This isn't what you think it is. He gave me his necklace. So.

SPEED DATE
Janet Allard

The facilitator of a community center speed-dating event welcomes a quirky group of people looking for love on Valentines Day, but betrays some mixed feelings about speed-dating in the process.

LAURA. Welcome Speed Daters! To our special Valentine's Day Speedy Chance for Love, here at the Mandandantanack Community Center.

I know you're all here tonight because you're (losers) I mean looking. Sorry. Looking for love and compassion, or maybe just a (hottie) I mean, date. I'm sure, if you're like me, you already lead a (worthless), sorry, wonderful life. Still, you've come here, brave souls that you are, searching for further (befuddlement) I mean fulfillment. Maybe you're looking for someone to (compete with) I mean, complete your already full life. I know (sexually) I mean secretly you're eyeing everyone in the room thinking is he (insane?) I mean, right for me. Maybe you're thinking, I need someone who can be a (Freak) I mean (Freudian) I mean Friend, as well as a (Sugar daddy) I mean, companion.

After all, nothing can compare to the joy of another (Persian), (Fireman), I mean person.

Excuse me, for misspeaking. I must be (hopeless) sorry, (loveless) no. Nervous.

I know you're all (weird) pardon me, wondering.

Will I ever meet someone I actually like?

Let alone love.

And how will I know when I meet this person?

And are they in this (entire loveless universe) I mean room?

And can true love really happen in the time it takes to boil angel hair pasta?

Well. You're not alone.

You've come to the right place.

A TINY MIRACLE WITH A FIBEROPTIC UNICORN
A somewhat nostalgic, sentimental comedy in two acts
Don Zolidis

Grandma Skolowski, who's a little off-her-rocker and speaks with a British accent, recounts a story from her youth that probably didn't happen.

(GRANDMA SKOLOWSKI speaks in a very sweet, very soft voice, with a British accent acquired from Masterpiece Theatre.)

GRANDMA SKOLOWSKI. When I was thirteen years old a man came up to me on the street and asked if he could see my legs. This was a very strange proposition at that time, but I thought I had wonderful legs so I showed him and he said those are some pretty stunning legs. I was quite flattered. In those days, if a man said something nice to you you were obligated to marry him. But I was thirteen so I couldn't marry him and besides he was more attracted to my brother Joseph but I didn't know there were such men at the time. And he said he could get me an audition for the Rockettes. Imagine me, dancing for the Rockettes. So I said I'd love to be in the Rockettes, so he gave me a ticket on the train and I went to New York City, and I went straight to Radio City Music Hall for my audition. And there I was in front of the producer, Howard Shulz and he said how old are you and I said thirteen and he said I was nineteen and I said no I'm thirteen and he said are you sure you're thirteen? And then I said I might be nineteen and he said you're hired. My parents knew nothing about this. They thought I was in Poland for girl scout camp. So I started dancing and let me tell you it was the best time of my life. Fifty girls—they were my family. We used to go skinny dipping in the East River. That was before the East River was discovered to be poisonous. We had a girl die. Esther was her name and she was from Iowa and she had huge knockers. I used to think everyone in Iowa had huge knockers until I went there one time and discovered it wasn't true, that no one in Iowa looked anything like Esther, which is why she left I suppose. Anyway, she drank some of the water and died which was a shame because she was the girl on my left. For the 1930 Christmas show we decided we were going to release live doves at the end of the dance. Don't ask me why. Well it so happened that someone forgot to feed the doves and they all died in their cages. The cages were over our heads so when they released the doves, we just heard plop plop plop as their carcasses rained from the sky. They were landing on us. I got hit in the shoulder which hurt because it was a rather large bird with talons and a beak. Mary on my right got hit right in the head and it knocked her out cold. I didn't know what to do. I started shouting, Mary's dead! Mary's dead! All the while more birds are dropping from the sky and the other girls are trying to continue the kickline. I thought that was the most absurd thing ever because if a girl is dead no one wants to see live girls dancing any more. Well maybe some people do, but I think those people are wrong. Mary lived. But we didn't use birds any more after that.

FEMALE DRAMA

ANTIGONE

adapted by David Rush

from Sophocles' classic play

Antigone has defied the order sent out by King Creon that her brother's body lie unburied, since (in Creon's mind) he died a traitor. Believing the gods' edict that all bodies be purified in burial is more important than Creon's law, Antigone goes ahead and buries him. When she is caught, she is sentence to be buried alive. Here she speaks to her sister about her fate.

ANTIGONE. You're going to finish making me ready. Creon will send his guard. Six men to guard one small woman. The gods will be laughing. They will take me to the cave prepared for me. Food and water for a day. A candle or two. They will leave me there. They will roll a magnificent stone over the opening and seal it shut. For a time, I will sit there in the cold and the dark. Then I will light a candle and eat and drink what they've left me, finishing it off in a hurry to get it over with. I will sleep with terrible dreams. After a while I will go hungry. Thirsty. I'll start to call out and weep and try to scratch my way through the rock. I will beg Creon to forgive me; I will promise to do whatever he wants me to. And worse: I will see my brothers and imagine they are laughing at me. I will talk to our father and imagine that he disowns me. I will cry out for help from Athena, from Zeus, from all the gods I can name and the sounds of my thin, hollow voice will die away without even an echo. I will grow weaker. Soon I won't even be able to stand. Then I will sleep. Then I will sleep. Forever.

ANTIGONE NOW

Melissa Cooper

inspired by Sophocles' *Antigone*

Ismene's sister Antigone was executed for burying the body of her brother Polyneices, named a traitor for battling his brother Eteocles for the throne. As Ismene mourns Antigone, she tries to rebuild her life as the city is rebuilt in the aftermath of the war.

ISMENE. Little sister, my little fish. Where are you now? Where did you go? Who will curl up beside me with her head in my lap? Who will scratch for a story to soothe her to sleep? Come back, little one, come back.

I hid in the room the day you were born. I saw you open your mouth and suck your first breath. Me. I was the one. Not Polyneices. Not Eteocles. Me. You never knew that before.

Polyneices is buried now. I'm all that's left. Only me to keep on. But I have no family and nothing to hold onto.

Did you know a whole crowd of people was waiting by the road? They wanted to cheer you when you walked out of your prison in triumph. It might have happened. There's so much that might have happened.

It's quiet now. In another minute, the sun will crack through the night sky and the people will go about their usual business: eating, working, fighting, playing, cooking, buying and selling.

Wait. Sssh. Did you hear that? It's a jackhammer. And that. A truck mixing cement. They've started to rebuild.

I want to see it. I want to watch them clear the rubble, stone by stone, and see the buildings rise.

How can I resist life? I can't. I can't resist life.

THE AUDITION
Don Zolidis

While preparing for the show, Carrie reflects on an early experience in the theatre. She speaks directly to the audience.

CARRIE. Okay. My life: by Carrie. My life is the most wonderful thing.

(She stops.)

My life is the…when I was ten years old I got cast in the school play. We were doing this play our teacher wrote about Winnie the Pooh. I was Tigger. Probably because I was pretty hyper. I even got to sing a song about Tiggers. I was so excited I stayed after school every day, and I learned my lines in the first week, and every night at home I'd sing my song about Tiggers and how they were made out of rubber and everything. Our school didn't have a lot of money, but my friend's Mom made me a costume and we had a lot of fun. And I felt really good about it. I mean, I felt…amazing. It was like my whole life I was looking for something I was good at, and then all of a sudden here it was, I was good at being Tigger. I couldn't run fast, I wasn't good at math, I couldn't even spell, but when I sang that Tigger song, I was proud. So the day of the show came, and I was backstage in my Tigger costume, and I was really nervous, I had to pee like every five minutes, and then I went out there on the stage, and the lights were really bright, and I could see the outline of all these heads out there, and I could hear them, and I did my song—and I just put everything I had into it, and I wasn't nervous any more, I was happy, and when I finished…the whole audience applauded for me. For me. I had never been applauded for anything my whole life. And then after the show, all the parents were coming up and hugging their kids, even the kids who played trees, I remember this Dad came up and he was like, "you were the most realistic tree of all of them" and everyone was there. And everyone was getting hugged. And there were all these flowers. And I looked around for my Mom…and I kept looking around for her…and I kept looking. And then everyone started to go home. And I was still there. And I was still in that stupid Tigger costume. I asked her later why she didn't come to my show, and she said, "what show?" *(Pause.)*

I was really good, too.

Black Butterfly, Jaguar Girl, Piñata Woman and Other Superhero Girls, Like Me

by Luis Alfaro

based on the writings of Alma Elene Cervantes, Sandra C. Muñoz, and Marisela Norté

Dolores joins a chorus of girls sharing moments of great change in their lives by talking about her father's death.

DOLORES. Today, my father died.

The whole day, I could tell something was wrong. When I asked why my father was in the hospital, my mother told me it was because he had a very bad cold. I had many colds, and I had never been taken to the hospital.

Plus, the whole day I kept hearing people whispering. When they finally told me that he had died, I didn't know what to do.

The last time I saw my Dad, was the day he picked me up in his orange Nova to go to his AA meeting with him. I always liked going to my Dad's AA meetings because there would always be coffee and donuts to eat, even though, sometimes, it was a little bit boring to have to hear all the people talk about how they didn't drink anymore. Which is why I couldn't understand why my father had died from alcoholism.

My family told me he died bleeding inside and the doctors couldn't help him.

But I didn't understand because my father was a "recovering" alcoholic. I always heard my Mom say that my Dad was sick because he had fought in the war.

I don't know if that was true, but I know fighting in the war didn't affect the way he treated me.

He was always good to me.

But today my Dad died.

And now he's gone.

CHARMING PRINCES

Emily C.A. Snyder

We all know Cinderella ran away from Prince Charming...but now we know why. This Cinderella wants more than just fairy tales and designer shoes—she wants a true love that doesn't mind a little dirt. Even if that means you've got to lose the shoes.

CINDERELLA. Fairy Godmother, listen to me, for just a moment—really *listen*. Do you know what last night was like? It was—it was everything you said it was. It was beautiful and perfect, and the music played and the chandeliers shone. And Prince Charming whirled me in his arms and I felt as light as a feather. And his kiss—well, that was kind of wet and swamp-like—but still! It was a *real* kiss, from a real prince, and it was kind of wonderful.

And he told me how beautiful I was as I stood there in the moonlight. And I thought I would die of happiness. But I didn't die of happiness—because it suddenly occurred to me that I wasn't happy. Oh, he was everything I'd hoped for—handsome, debonair—but that's *all* he was: handsome. Charming. And that was all I would ever be to him: beautiful, with moonlight in my hair. But what would happen when midnight struck? When the spell faded?

So I tried to tell him what I was thinking, and he told me not to speak. And I tried to tell him that he was under a spell, that it was all just fairy dust and moonlight and champagne and that if he *really* saw me, *really* saw me as I am—here, in the ashes, in my daily life, that he wouldn't love me at all. That I'd be no more desirable than...than a frog. But he just kissed me a second time, and told me not to *think*. So I threw my shoe at his head and ran away.

DIARY OF A TEENAGE GIRL

by Marielle Heller

adapted from the graphic novel by Phoebe Gloeckner

Minnie Goetze, an honest and curious 15-year-old in 1976, has just had her first sexual experience, and still doesn't know how she feels about it. She dictates to her tape-recorded diary via a microphone, recalling one of her first loves from oh so long ago (when she was 13).

MINNIE. I'm not exactly in love with him either, you know. I'm anticipating that I should like to listen to these tapes in a decade or so, reminiscing over my wild teenage-hood. Maybe I'll even let my husband hear. I'm not going to destroy this diary. The last one, I tore the pages out and ripped them up into tiny pieces and flushed them down the toilet. That was in eighth grade and I was in love with Sarah S. at Hamlin School for Girls. I wanted, so many times, to kiss her. I liked to imagine Sarah in a dreadful accident, falling off the roof of the school while she was playing basketball. *(MINNIE picks up the stuffed animal and cradles it in her arms as if it were Sarah.)* I would run down the cement stairs to the landing where she lay bleeding and hold her in my arms and kiss her and tell her I loved her. Then she would die, but not before responding to my kiss with a breathless last remark, "Oh, I love you too, how I love you—I have always loved you." *(MINNIE kisses the stuffed animal passionately.)* We were thirteen then.

FACE FORWARD
Growing Up in Nazi Germany
Brendon Votipka

November, 1938. Nuremberg, Germany. Rebecca attempts to sort out recent events, afraid that rumors of internment camps may be true. Though scattered, she puts on a brave face and tries to not let her emotions get the best of her as she reaches out to her dearest friend, the audience.

REBECCA. I had a nightmare. But when I woke up, it wasn't a nightmare at all. I've just been dreaming about everything that's happened.

All over Germany and Austria there were riots for two days. I stayed in at home, sleeping on the floor of my parents' room. I felt like a child to be so afraid, but the destruction is horrible.

In the night, homes and businesses were destroyed. The Synagogue we go to was burnt to the ground by the SS soldiers. They say every synagogue in Germany is destroyed. In some cities the Hitler youth were involved in the attacks. Boys younger than me.

The watch shop and the bakery on our street have the windows bashed in. Further into town you really see the destruction. As you walk around you find pieces of glass, shards of the windows from the homes of Jews. My mother and father are trying to count how many of their friends have been taken away. They're calling it Kristallnacht. The Night of Broken Glass.

Apparently, some Polish Jew killed a diplomat and the Nazis sent word that it was time to attack.

I don't want to go to school anymore, but my Father says I have to. He thinks the routine is important to making me feel safe and normal.

A girl at my school was talking about Kristallnacht and said thousands and thousands of Jews were taken away on trains. To go work at camps. But we don't really know what happens there.

My father is a locksmith, and builds locks for his job. I always felt safe at home because he has the best locks on our house. Those locks let me sleep well every night.

Now I'm afraid that locks aren't going to keep the Nazis out. Locks won't help.

THE FINAL ROSE
Bekah Brunstetter

Beatrice, a contestant on The Bachelor, has just been let go by her Bachelor, whom she truly has fallen in love with. Before her sad limo departure, Beatrice gets one last chance to talk to the camera.

BEATRICE. I'm kind of just in shock.
I mean, I really—I really—

> *(Pause.)*

It just hurts, you know?
Love. Like really. Like it really happened.
We didn't expect it to.
Like—you start with their eyebrows.
Not how much you want to do it with them or how much they seem to fit your life or your agenda, or whatever. You start with something small—a very small thing like the shape of their fingernails or the sound of their voice.
And it grows from there in the kind of way that you can't help or stop.
And it isn't calculated. And it isn't planned.
And then it rushes you and before you know it you're totally there, like you've moved all your stuff there, and set up a home there and changed your mailing address to there and you don't even know it.
Being in—love.

> *(She starts to feel like a douchebag but she keeps talking.)*

You—change your address. To it.
You set up utilities and unpack your—
You put your stuff on the walls.
You're just there. You live there now. And you can't even remember moving. You're just there.

> *(Beat.)*

I just really—I mean, like—for real—

> *(Pause. She can no longer speak, so she looks out the window at the rain. Tears gather in her eyes.*
> *The lights burn on her.*
> *Then suddenly, dark.)*

HIROSHIMA: CRUCIBLE OF LIGHT
Robert Lawson

A woman recalls her drive through Hiroshima after the bombing.

> *(She glances up at the audience, then looks down at her lap to gather her thoughts, trying to find a way to communicate something very painful to her. Finally, she looks out at the audience. She tells a story, but it is increasingly clear as she goes along that she is having trouble maintaining the pretense that this is not about her.)*

WOMAN IN THE WHEELCHAIR. I will tell you the story of a woman. A woman who found herself in an unfamiliar town.

There were glimpses of the town that seemed somehow familiar, but she could not say why. In her pocket, she found a map—and yet the map seemed to be of some other place—or else another time, terribly out-of-date now, rendered worthless by a somehow forgotten circumstance.

She looked around her, and she sensed that familiar roads had disappeared, and that mountains she had loved had been miraculously and ruthlessly reduced to rubble. Of course, in a way, she did not really miss the details that had vanished from the map, since she was now a stranger to these parts…and she was lost.

It was a town vacant of buildings, whose broad avenues were populated only by heroic statues, clad all in white, captured in mid-stride, fingers pointing to the four directions. There were mechanisms lining the avenues, set in cement, all unmoving and yet somehow threatening, and so she tucked the map away in a pocket close to the heart as if it were a bulletproof vest.

> *(Beat. Shift out of metaphor—)*

When you are driving, secure in your little box, you forget that you are hurtling through space, hurling your fragile body into the unknown. What is around that corner? Sometimes—I've noticed this—I can be driving and suddenly realize that I don't know exactly how I got where I am—this particular curve in the road, this particular bridge—because my mind has drifted, and I have been driving by habit. Unconscious habit.

When you are driving, secure in your little box, and you forget that you are hurtling your fragile body into the unknown, did you ever wonder if anyone else has drifted, like you have drifted, and is driving simply from habit? Unaware and unseeing? Did you ever wonder that?

(She drags herself back into her story, back into metaphor.)

The ever-present rain was tapping its codes and patterns, conspiring to distract her from finding her way.

How will she decipher the ghosts in the folds and the symbols in the legend of the map?

Well, perhaps gravity would provide a clue to her location.

(She tries to stand, almost as if she had forgotten she could not— and crumples onto the stage floor. Beat. She stares at her useless legs.)

IRENA'S VOW

Dan Gordon

based on the life of Irena Gut Opdyke

Irena Gut is a nineteen-year-old Polish Catholic girl who has hidden twelve Jews in the basement of a German Major without his knowledge. Now she has been informed that one of the married women is pregnant. Because Irena was trained as a nurse, the Jews want her to perform an abortion, knowing it would be suicidal to deliver a baby in the basement within earshot of the Major upstairs...

IRENA. No... This is not just a matter of religion. I saw a baby... ripped out of its mother's arms and killed in front of me while I stood by and I did nothing... I could do nothing... And I saw the mother of that baby shot to death in front of me and I could do nothing. And I made a vow to God then and there that if I ever got the chance to save a life I would do it. That's why without even thinking I took you here to hide you. Because of that vow... But I was wrong. You were right.

(She looks at IDA.)

And you have taught me that... It isn't enough just to save a life...to preserve a heartbeat...to simply survive... We have to live... We have to live in the face of death, otherwise, the Hitlers and the Rokitas of the world have won and have turned us into, what did you call it, Lazar?

(She crosses to LAZAR and searches his eyes.)

...rats in the darkness? Isn't that what you said? That we couldn't just be rats living in the darkness?

(She turns back to IDA.)

If there were no Hitler...no Sturmbannfurher, no Ghettos, no camps, no S.S., no Major Rugemer upstairs, would you keep this baby?

[IDA says yes.]

Then I'll have no part of this. Hitler's not going to get this baby.

[LAZAR begins to protest.]

(IRENA *speaks with the conviction of a Joan of Arc who has just heard her voices tell her she will free France.*)

No, I believe God brought you to me and to this hiding place. This was no accident. And maybe it was for this very reason so that this baby could be born and that this child should live... God would never allow any harm to come to us because of this baby.

LAST NIGHT IN LONDON
Kimberly Lew

High school students lament their last night in London as a part of a summer study abroad program. Asked to fill out a survey about their experiences, everyone addresses questions about their time in a foreign country. When asked what she learned from her time abroad, Jill shares a valuable lesson from her travels.

JILL. My roommates and I went to Rome for a few days during our 'travel break' midway through the program. And the city was beautiful, the food was amazing. We saw the pantheon and the Trevi fountain and I felt like I was Audrey Hepburn in *Roman Holiday*. But the one thing I wasn't expecting was how friendly the boys were there. Everywhere we went there were these cute Italian boys with their dark hair and eyes calling, "Bella, bella." A girl could get used to that, right? Anyway, there was one boy in particular, Angelo, and he started talking to us while we were sitting in a little cafe. He ended up showing us around the city, and I thought to myself: how romantic, wait until I tell my friend back at home about this beautiful Italian boy I met while I was abroad. He even gave me a little kiss before we parted and I got home with butterflies in my stomach… until I looked in my purse and saw that my wallet was gone. Yes, completely gone. And that was when I learned my greatest lesson here: never trust a boy. No matter what country you're in, they'll steal whatever they can take from you.

LEAH'S TRAIN

Karen Hartman

Leah's family has a chance to flee from Russia, but before they can go, Leah must roam the country by train alone to find her nephew and her younger brother. In the midst of her harrowing journey, she imagines what it would be like to reunite with them.

LEAH. Borukh. My train was freezing. Bumpy. Filthy and dark. So slow I could have walked. We rode through woods and burnt towns, around and around and around. The guards yelled, "Inspection," and I would lie in a ditch all night. I hate dirt. Once I got back on the train and my legs were crawly with worms. An hour journey took a day, a day journey took a week, and in this way I looked for you a month. But now it's over. Little brother. Come into my arms and rest.

> (LEAH *holds out her arms and closes her eyes. She opens them and checks her bag.*)

Yosele, I slap you for taking him away. I beat your face with a stick. Crack! For your sneaky ways. Crack! For Rivke's tears. Crack crack crack for taking my brother and leaving me behind.

No, Leah.

Yosele. Borukh. Such a miracle to see you both. No stories of the train, no. My suffering was for the family's good. Let us sit still and recall my generous ways.

God if you let me find them I'll make any sacrifice you say. I won't go to America, I'll stay behind. Well I'll go, but I'll do a lot of good there. Please let them be in Simferopol. Please let them be in Simferopol. Please…

PATTY RED PANTS
Trista Baldwin

Patty Red Pants, at age fifteen, has heard of the recent murder of a girl her age, in the woods near her house. Both attracted and repelled by these same woods, Patty recalls a dream she had of running through their trees. As she recalls the dream, it becomes more and more real for her.

PATTY RED PANTS. I'm running through the woods. It's dark. But the stars are out, above the trees. I'm running in my nightgown, I'm running because I'm in love, I'm in love with everything, the world, and the ground is soft and my legs feel light, and my heart is pounding, and I'm running because I'm in love, I'm in love with everything, and I have to run, to—to breathe, for—for air, I have to run to burn—burn the love off me. The limbs of the trees lean towards me and the love keeps pounding and pounding and— I'm catching fire. My feet are on fire. The hair between my legs is flaming, my eyes are starting to burn, my hair is all fire, my chest— I'm going to burn down the trees, I'm going to burn *everything*.

(A dark figure approaches. She stops running.)

Then something came.

It took me with its teeth, it took me in its mouth, it wasn't afraid of my body, on fire. I think I am screaming, or trying to speak. But it is only part of my burning. It's carrying me in its mouth, through the trees. He's carrying me to the lake. (I can't remember.)

And I'm going under.

I'm going under.

I'm under water.

Now I can see myself, I'm floating, my nightgown is a balloon around me—everything is peaceful and quiet—there is such relief—relief not to be burning anymore.

(PATTY collapses. Lays breathing heavily on the floor.)

PERFECT SCORE
Katie Henry

Hannah, a smart but overly anxious high school senior, is in the middle of a college interview, and has just been asked why she wants to attend Yale University, her ultimate dream school.

HANNAH. That's like asking, "Why do you want to go to Heaven?" Not that I'm super religious, it was a bad simile, but…I've always wanted to go to Yale. My mom, um, my mom went there, for undergrad, and I remember when I was little I'd always see her walking around in her Yale sweatshirt, and she'd tell me all these stories about her amazing friends and crazy professors, and it just sounded so perfect. Yale was part of who she was, how many colleges can make that much an impact on someone? And…she, um, she died. When I was ten, she got hit by a drunk driver, and then she was just gone, because of some idiot with a car, and…I want to go to Yale because I want to have a family, again. I want to live with hundreds of brilliant people, and I want to feel wanted. I want to meet my mother's professors and walk up Science Hill and I want to stand where she stood. I miss her every day, and I want her to be proud of me. Maybe that isn't a good reason to want Yale. I should have told you I liked New Haven and the residential college system but…

REGINA FLECTOR WINS THE SCIENCE FAIR
A Ten-minute Play with Results and Conclusions
Marco Ramirez

Regina, an average student, has just entered the Science Fair up against kids who have infused their projects with their parents' time and money. After suffering from their very vocal criticism, she makes the case for her less-than-perfect presentation, proudly standing behind her work.

REGINA. —LOOOOK!

> *(Everyone stops. Everything stops. A beat.* REGINA *takes a breath and continues:)*

I'm—…
I'm not a great speaker, okay?
I'm not even a GOOD one, really,
but I worked really hard on this and it wasn't easy and and and my mom works a lot and my dad—,
He's not really…as "involved" as your dads and he doesn't—,
He doesn't know how to use PowerPoint—…
And my sister's kinda always doing her own thing, so, it might not be much, but it's *all me*, okay?
This is *all*—…
Like you know how they say "do your best", and we're all like "okay" and we think we mean it?
We say it but there's always something, you know, something you could've done a little better?
Well.
Not here.
I've *never* meant it before.
You've said it and I've said it but I never meant it before.
And I mean it now:
This
Is
My best.
This is… This is really, really honestly—…

And when I couldn't use tomato sauce I used ketchup
And when I ran out of glue I used scotch tape
And when I ran out of scotch tape I used chewing gum
(Hence the ants)
And no one was there to proofread everything I had written so it's
probably full of typos,
Typos I would LOVE to correct, but, no one told me,
So fine,
No, I didn't.
Not yet.
'Cause this is me.
This is no one else.
Just. Me.
And I might not be that smart and it might stink and be the worst
science project you've ever seen—

—But I don't care.
'Cause I know that no matter what you think of it—…
I don't care.
I mean, I CARE, sure, but not really.
'Cause I'm…
'Cause right now…?
I'm really, REALLY, proud of myself…
And I don't care about the blue ribbon or the red ribbon or the anything
ribbon, I just—…

> (A beat. REGINA *takes a final breath. She stands taller than she*
> *ever has before. With confidence:*)

Detergent A worked better, okay?
And I—…

> (A beat.
> *Proudly:*)

I figured that out on my own.

SEVEN MINUTES IN HEAVEN
Steven Levenson

Phoebe is popular. A high school freshman, she's pretty and likeable and always perfectly upbeat. Underneath the surface, however, things are not so straightforward. Here, Phoebe talks about her childhood and the inner wounds that she has learned to cover up so convincingly.

PHOEBE. Phil Marnell has a scar. It's tiny. You wouldn't even really see it unless you knew it was there and you were looking for it. It's from chicken pox and it's on his left temple and it's a little dot like somebody stamped him with a dot when he was born so that they would always be able to find him.

When I was ten, my dad quit his job so he could find out what he really wanted to do, and it started to look like what he really wanted to do was watch TV in his boxers and drink Diet Rite. My mom would come home at seven and I would be in my room and they would fight. My mom would yell and my dad would cry, and then my *dad* would yell and my mom would cry, and then my dad would curl up in a ball and rock himself back and forth and say the word, "please," over and over, until it didn't even sound like a word but more like a sound that an animal might make.

I used to sit in my closet on a pile of dirty clothes and push myself in against the door and wait for everything to stop. Sometimes my mom would leave and she wouldn't come back for a few hours. Or a few days. Sometimes my dad would say sorry and they would make up and we all had dinner together and Dad put pants on and everybody smiled, and those times were the worst. Sometimes I would sit there in the dark and I would imagine I wasn't really there or that somebody far away was dreaming me and what if they woke up. Sometimes I would take my fingernail and I would stretch it across my chest very slowly, so that the skin would begin to split and a little inch of blood would open into my shirt and then everything would get very quiet and I didn't cry and I wasn't scared and I felt alone and emptied out and like maybe I would never die, but even if I did it would be ok.

(Beat.)

My dad would just keep saying, "please," until my mom left the room and then he would say, "love isn't free, Betsy. It costs you. It always costs you. It always costs you."

It always costs you.

SHE LIKE GIRLS
Chisa Hutchinson

At the urging of her English teacher, Mr. Keys, Kia has decided to attend her first LGBT support group meeting. Here she finally vents about the horrific things that have happened since she's come out in her dangerously homophobic community.

KIA. Hi, everybody. My name is Kia. I'm… I never been to one of these things before, so I'm a little nervous…I guess I'm here because there's been a lot of fucked up things goin' on—I'm sorry, can I say that?—yeah…just a whole lot of stuff…

(Beat.)

I…I have a girlfriend. She's my first girlfriend. My first anything, actually. I used to think that I just wasn't interested in bein' wit' anybody in that way 'cause I couldn't think of any *guy* I wanted to be wit' like that…and my mom was happy about that 'cause she said I should be concentrating on my schoolwork anyway. Which is kinda funny 'cause it was som'n I read in class that first put the idea in my head that I… that I could actually do this, you know? I never did thank you for that, Mr. Keys… Anyway, my girl's mom just kicked her out and she's stayin' with us now. My mother don't even know for sure that we together, but she still 'on't want me to sleep in the same room as her, which is kinda stupid when you think about it 'cause her face is all like…

(Choking up a little:)

…swollen and bruised and shit from her mom…she can't even… she can't even lay on the pillow without it hurtin' so…all that hot lesbian love that my mom think might go down is definitely out of the question…I just found out that my best friend is an even bigger gay-basher than I was forgiving his ass for bein' in the first place. He done some shit lately that I honestly never woulda thought he was capable of… I'm just wonderin' what I'm supposed to do now? Now that I'm out on this limb, what am I supposed to do to keep from falling off it? Especially wit' everybody shakin' the damn tree like this.

TO KNOW KNOW KNOW ME
Courtney Baron

Mariah is a teenager who thought her family was getting a new lease on life when they moved into a nicer apartment in a new neighborhood. Just after her move, she's woken up in the middle of the night, and told to go to the next door neighbor's house. Her brother is in big trouble with the law, and the good change, well, it doesn't seem like it's going to be so good after all.

MARIAH. *(Suddenly:)* I don't want to go to school. I said it last night, right before I got in bed. I don't want to go to school. I don't know why I said it. But I did and my ma, you know, she just says, "You got to." Nothing else but that. And all night I'm laying in bed, thinking, I don't want to go to school. And then it's like 3:30 in the morning, I know cuz I look at the clock. And I hear my ma and she's talking softly. And then, I hear her coming down the hall. She's coming to get me, I think. I don't know why, it's just this feeling I have. And so I just, I don't know. I just get up and put on some clothes. Just throw them on. And I'm right, because the next I know she's knocking on my door, she's saying, "Baby, come on out." And I don't know why I don't want to, but I don't. And I do it any way and she's standing there. I see she's crying. Or at least real sad. And she says, "Baby, you got to go over to the neighbors." I don't think I should ask why. I feel like she's gonna tell me if she can. So, I go back in my room and put on my shoes and grab a few things, like my phone, and my book bag. And then I go down the hall. My brother is standing there. He's got this funny look on his face. He tries to smile at me, but it looks like it hurts too much for him to do it. My ma pulls me next to her and says, "Baby, your brother did something big." And I don't know by how she's saying if he won the lottery or shot somebody. He's still not smiling really, so I figure it's not the lottery, right? He'd be smiling if it was the lottery. So, then I start to hear all of these cars pulling out front the building. And you hear all these people talking and then there are cops coming out of our kitchen. They don't look too mad or scared, so I don't know. Then my brother comes up to me and he says, "I done something big, because I had to." And the cops are talking to my ma, but I can't quite get an ear in to hear it. And my ma comes over to me, she gives me like 40 bucks from her wallet. She says, "This is for today and tomorrow, the neighbors are expecting you. I'll be back before you know it, but I can't leave you here alone." She says, "They have a kid named Cory, he's the same grade as you." And then she asks one of the cops to take me over to his apartment. We moved in three days ago. Moved to a bigger spot than before. Felt so nice. Didn't have to share a bathroom anymore, two bathrooms. My ma and me sharing one. My brother with his nasty habits, so dirty like all boys, get the other. And my room was a little bigger. And I don't know. It all seemed good. And now this. And now it all changes.

WHAT I WANT TO SAY BUT NEVER WILL
Alan Haehnel

This monologue and all other aspects of What I Want to Say But Never Will *are based on responses the playwright received from middle and high school students across the country. He asked students to respond anonymously to three questions: What is something you want to say but think you never will? To whom to you wish you could say it? Why do you think you can't say it?*

#58. Dad, I know you and Mom had to divorce. I remember the fights when I was five, Mom throwing wine bottles at you, you throwing vases back at her. The divorce was horrible, but it had to happen. But what I need to know is…do you love me? Part of me says of course you do; I'm your daughter! But when you e-mail me, the few times you do, you write such short little notes. I mean, couldn't you spare more than three syllables to let me know I'm important to you? And really, is your schedule so busy or gas so expensive that you couldn't make even one of my soccer games? And when we come to visit for the two weeks every summer, don't you want to do something with us, your daughters, besides put us to work? Couldn't you take just a minute to call me on my birthday? This year I waited almost all day for your call. Maybe you think I just know that you love me; you don't have to tell me or show me. Maybe you think I'm fine without you. I'm not. Every day a green truck comes down our street, Dad, and even though my brain knows it's not you, my heart can't help hoping, day after day, that it will turn into the driveway and it will be you. Every day I'm hurt when it's not you. Maybe I should be flattered that you think I'm old enough and independent enough to get along fine on my own. You certainly seem to be fine without me. Are you fine without me? Do you miss me, ever? Dad, I'm not old enough; I don't think I'll ever be old enough not to want to have you hug me and cheer for me and talk to me! Talk to me! Tell me! I'll never be old enough not to need you to tell me you love me. You love me, your daughter, you love me.

MALE OR FEMALE COMEDY

DARCY'S CINEMATIC LIFE
Christa Crewdson

Darcy, a self proclaimed semi-outcast, shares fears and strategies for an upcoming field trip to the museum: having to find just the right seat on the bus, a group to hang with, and a way to make it through the day.

DARCY. Not much has changed since then. It's like that movie Groundhog Day. Every school day is the same. Liza is mean to me, Chad ignores me and I try to find ways to amuse myself in this institution of monotony. Anyway, I have to confess that for the first time in my life I am grappling with a problem. A teen problem. I am after all only human, as much as I hate to admit it. I'm talking about the impending class trip to the art museum. Now I know you might think a field trip to the museum is no big deal but to a slightly different, semi-outcast like myself, it is a major deal. There are many critical factors: 1) Who you sit next to on the bus. It's a long ride, not to mention everyone will be judging who you sit with. 2) Finding a group to hang with for the day. This strategy is a little more difficult. My normal strategy is to stand close enough to an "accepted group" to look like I am with them, but not close enough for them to know I am there. To an outside observer it appears that I am part of the group. This requires extreme concentration, extreme planning...

THE DOG LOGS

CJ Johnson

Savoir-Faire is a very earnest, very loyal, very dedicated and very focused two-year-old professional racing greyhound.

SAVOIR-FAIRE. All my life, all I've wanted to do is catch that damn rabbit.

Every now and then I find myself penned up and then BANG there's that damn rabbit and all I want to do is grab it by its throat and shake it and kill it and gobble it up. But it's so *fast*. I mean I reckon I'm really super fast but it's faster. It just seems to be faster than me. In fact it just seems to be faster than all of us, me and all the other dogs I seem to find myself running around with.

I also know that if I ever catch that rabbit I'm going to make my master really happy. He wants me to catch that rabbit as much as I do. I can see it in his eyes as I'm chasing that rabbit.

I think the rabbit's name is Fred. I'm not sure why. Maybe I just heard that somewhere sometime.

It's funny, when I'm chasing that rabbit, all I can think of is, "Catch the rabbit. Catch the rabbit. Catch the rabbit." Partly because my master always seems to forget to feed me for a couple of days before he sends me after that rabbit. Instead he comes and says to me, "Catch the rabbit. Catch the rabbit. Catch the rabbit." Like I don't already want to catch that stupid rabbit!

Sometimes I have dreams about that rabbit. They can be good or bad dreams. In the good dreams, I catch up to the rabbit, and I grab it by its leg and then I grab it by its throat and shake it and kill it and gobble it up. In the bad dreams, that stupid rabbit outruns me again. Man I want to catch that rabbit.

I'm Not Ebenezer Scrooge!

Tim Kochenderfer

It's Christmas Eve and Carter has just been dumped by Ella. The two had been dating for four years and Ella was expecting an engagement ring, but what she got for Christmas instead was a very high tech garbage can. Ella storms off after a huge fight.

CARTER. *(Yells after* ELLA:*)* Yeah?! Go ahead walk away! Yeah, yeah go ahead and get in your car! Yeah, that's right, you turn that key and put it in reverse! Yeah, yeah go ahead, slam into my mailbox! That's right, run right over it! Yeah back up so you hit it again! Real mature. Yeah okay you do that, you go ahead and set the wreckage on fire, yeah, yeah go ahead! Yeah, yeah you just keep driving! Keep driving! Yeah go ahead, drive on my lawn! Yeah, yeah that's right, you do that, you go ahead and spin the tires so it tears up the sod. Yeah, yeah that's fine! That's fine! Go ahead and take that salt out of your trunk. Yeah, you go right on ahead and salt my flower beds so nothing will ever grow in them again! Yeah, that's right drive off! Just drive off! Yeah, yeah okay yeah, go ahead back up. Back up into my driveway. Yeah, you go ahead, go ahead and get out of your car, yeah, just add more salt to my flower beds, yeah go ahead, just salt them up! Yeah, go ahead, speed off! Yeah that's right! Who needs you!

VOLLEYGIRLS
Rob Ackerman

*At a high school girls' volleyball game, a magical Russian Referee stops
time in the middle of an argument with a coach, steps down from his/her
place at the net, and offers a unique perspective on sports and on life.*

REF. *(To us:)* This fight with me is desperate attempt of Coach to
motivate failing team. I know this. Coach knows this. Is game he must
play to teach players to play. But wait, I want show you something,
is very interesting. *(Climbs down from the perch.)* Look here. You see
this girl, you see how she sits on heels, not toes. This not only body
language, is language of the soul. This tells me she not believe. This
why coach fights with me. Okay, watch now. Here comes ball. Watch
in slow motion. This you cannot see with naked eye. Here, right here,
at this moment, she turn away, just little bit, just tiny moment, takes
eye off ball. See? You see this? This is fear. This is doubt. This is lack
of confidence. She should have big round eyes like jungle cat. Bright.
Burning. She does not. She does not know this, but when she is not
believing, she is literally not seeing. And this happens so fast, faster
than blink of eye. This is saddest thing in all of sports. And is true in
every sport, not just this one. In life, also. *(Returns to position.)* Okay.
Enough. I am finished. Sorry to interrupt your theatre.

MALE OR FEMALE DRAMA

ACTS OF GOD

Mark Rigney

Two weeks after a tornado destroys her trailer park home, Toni (or Tony) Strader describes searching for and finding her (or his) missing dog, Skunk.

TONI/TONY. Me, I went to the counselors like first thing. "Crisis counselors," they call 'em. They were everywhere. Some from whole other counties. I sat down, I was like, "I don't care 'bout my trailer, that's only stuff, what's gone is gone, but Skunk"—he's a whole 'nother story. I got him when I was eight. He was just a puppy. Hadn't even named him yet when he ran down a real skunk. And my puppy, he *stank.* And then *I* stank, the *trailer* stank, my *mom*—everything. It's no good havin' a stinky mom; it's like the opposite of what you want, right? And Skunk! You ever given a dog a bath in pure vinegar? It's been what, six years?—and I still can't deal with salad dressing. But Skunk, he's fine now. Look, here's a picture—exactly like the one I was posting all over, tryin' to get him back. Community boards, telephone poles, everywhere. But he was just gone. No barking, nothing. The Humane Society didn't have him, Animal Control didn't have him, the neighbors—hey, what neighbors, right? Where I live, that word is like irrelevant. 'Course, I don't live there now. I live in a shelter. Future Homeless of America, that's me! But then, eight days after the storm, I see this thing in the paper. They've got dogs they picked up way out in *[insert town]*, and they're tryin' to figure out who they go with. My mom and me, we drive out, and there's Skunk, in this stainless steel kennel. I know it's not real normal, but I couldn't even wait for him to come out. I went in. I lay down with Skunk in that tiny little kennel and nobody could get me out for like a full half hour. He's with us in the shelter now. Shares my cot. I think maybe everything's gonna mostly work out.

AIR GUITAR HIGH

Laura Schellhardt

Marvel, the wardrobe master for the US Regional Air Guitar Championships, is being interviewed for a documentary about the competition being produced by his (or her) classmates.

MARVEL. When I was young, I used to imagine I was Cyclops.
The comic book character. Not the Greek monster.
And not because he was the greatest comic book character in the world.
He was sort of awkward actually. His super power was absorbing ambient rays and converting them into optic blasts. Which loosely translated just means you can't look at anyone. Not directly anyway.
Because you'd incinerate them.

But I was sort of a shy kid.
So looking at people directly was… I don't know…
So maybe it struck me that we were alike in that way.
Or maybe it's because Cyclops was really good at geometry which I figured would make him good at pool and I always wanted to be good at pool, I thought it would make me… I don't know…

But what really drew me to Cyclops were his sunglasses.
They allowed him to control the optic rays, yeah, but they also meant he could look at anyone he wanted to. Directly.
That was the real power as far as I was concerned.
To be able to look people in the eyes without them being able to see into yours.

So I guess that's why I'm doing this. Because if you're gonna get up in front of all those people and make them see something that's not really there? Well, I think it takes someone a little superhuman to be able to do that.
Someone a little…Conan, maybe.
Or Gambit
Or Captain Marvel
Or…
Or…
Or…
I don't know…

Cyclops maybe.

HIROSHIMA: CRUCIBLE OF LIGHT
Robert Lawson

A denizen of New York City joins a chorus of people sharing their reactions to the bombing of Hiroshima.

CITY DWELLER. You want to know what I think? Look—I live in New York City. Sure, there's a lot of crime, lots of people get mugged every day—friends of mine. But what am I gonna do? Walk through every day fucking paranoid, afraid of my shadow? That's a lot of fun. No, basically I ignore it. I'm careful, sure I don't walk through the South Bronx at midnight flashing a wad of cash.

You know what I think? I think this nuclear thing's the same. Some military skinhead's sitting in some waterproof silo somewhere, chained to the wall, his finger poised on the button, probably stoned on something, probably acid or schrooms, something "mind illuminating" and easy to sneak in, easy to ingest, like smuggled in in a can of Spaghettios. So maybe one day he has a revelation that he's Jesus Christ or something and that the day of reckoning has come, and he does the deed. Then They do the deed, then We do the deed and then we're all done dead. Ask ya': whatt'm I gonna do about some skinhead hallucinator I never met who might push the button? Lose sleep? No.... Me? I just try and make sure I'm enjoying what I'm doing, in case it's the last thing I ever do on planet Earth.

The future? There is no such thing. *(Gestures around.)* This is it. Ain't nothin' more than this. This is it. Yeah…there is no more.

JUST LIKE I WANTED
Rebecca Schlossberg

Joey, a suicidal teenager, has just returned home from a long day of school and group therapy. As he (or she) plays make-believe with adorable little sister Haley, she reminds him (or her) that things could get better in time. Joey is swept up in this and contemplates what it would mean to be happy.

JOEY. And she was right.
At that moment I believed her.
For that one moment.
I felt that I actually could be happy.
Away from everything.
Everyone.
Just out on the beach.
Sitting by the water.
Washing my hands in the ocean.
Carving my name in the sand.
As the waves wash it away.
Digging my feet in the soft sand.
Soaking in the sun.
Not even looking back.
High school behind me.
Everything behind me.
Just me, all peaceful.
Cool.
Calm.
With nothing but the sun beaming down on me.
Laughing.
Laughing so much my chest would hurt.
Eating Oreos with peanut butter.
On the sands of the beach.
All peaceful.
Calm and cool.
Perfect.
And I'd be happy.
Perfectly happy.
Only happiness.
And nothing else.

RUMORS OF POLAR BEARS
Jonathan Dorf

Deme, 18, is a survivor of a climate change catastrophe. Along with her (or his) 15-year-old brother, Romulus, she (or he) has banded together with a few other teens to navigate the Mad Max-like landscape that's left. Deme shares a glimpse into her (or his) tragic memories with the audience.

DEME. The year Romulus turned three, I remember a man in a designer pin-striped suit and perfectly polished shoes swinging a sledgehammer at every inch of his Hummer, screaming that he would no longer be part of the problem. And when he's done, he sits on the curb and points at me to come closer and he says he wants to set it on fire, but he can't, because he just can't hurt the planet any more. He grabs my hand and starts to cry, and he says he's sorry he's crying, but he can't help it and isn't there some way he could give back the Hummer and the half hour showers for just one more minute with his wife? And then he stands up, wipes his face, tells me the Oil and Water Wars are all his fault, and throws himself onto the freeway below.

    (Beat.)

I made that up. Not the Hummer or the hammer or the crying or him taking my hand or the freeway. But the Oil and Water Wars didn't start for another week, and that's just what we call them now because there's nobody to tell us different.